Incarnate in Word and Song

Exploring Music in Liturgy and Life

Orin Johnson

LITURGICAL PRESS

Collegeville, Minnesota

www.litpress.org

1   2   3   4   5   6   7   8   9

Library of Congress Cataloging-in-Publication Data

Names: Johnson, Orin, author.
Title: Incarnate in word and song : exploring music in liturgy and life / Orin Johnson.
Description: Collegeville, Minnesota : Liturgical Press, [2023] | Includes bibliographical references. | Summary: "A close study of the interrelationship of scripture, liturgy, and liturgical music"— Provided by publisher.
Identifiers: LCCN 2022034577 (print) | LCCN 2022034578 (ebook) | ISBN 9780814667699 (trade paperback) | ISBN 9780814667705 (epub) | ISBN 9780814667705 (pdf)
Subjects: LCSH: Church music—Catholic Church. | Catholic Church—Liturgy. | BISAC: RELIGION / Christian Rituals & Practice / Worship & Liturgy | RELIGION / Christian Ministry / Pastoral Resources
Classification: LCC ML3002 .J65 2023 (print) | LCC ML3002 (ebook) | DDC 781.71/2—dc23/eng/20220722
LC record available at https://lccn.loc.gov/2022034577
LC ebook record available at https://lccn.loc.gov/2022034578

"Orin Johnson combines serious scholarship with the practical wisdom of thirty years in music ministry to highlight a topic that has long needed greater attention: the right relationship of the liturgical rite, music, and preaching. This accessible yet substantive book will help start an important conversation among the various liturgical ministries in worshiping communities."

—Ann M. Garrido, Associate Professor of Homiletics,
Aquinas Institute of Theology

"Moving beyond traditional studies of the role of music in the liturgy, Johnson's book explores what insights music and musical performance can bring to preaching. Johnson carefully shows his readers how preaching in our churches could be enriched if preachers incorporated basic insights from musical performance into their preaching. Reading at times like the work of a poet, the book is enriched by skillfully crafted examples that model attention to intonation, pacing, volume, and the need for silence. This book is a must read for all preachers and those studying preaching, as well as parish music ministers. It serves as a poignant reminder of the need for presiders, preachers, and other parish ministers to work in concert with one another to help our assemblies raise their hearts and voices to the Lord."

—Nathan P. Chase, Assistant Professor of Liturgical and
Sacramental Theology, Aquinas Institute of Theology,
St. Louis, Missouri

"Written for preachers, evangelizers, lovers of Scripture, and liturgical musicians alike, *Incarnate in Word and Song*, draws on Johnson's considerable experience as a liturgical musician and composer to highlight the connections between the Word and music in liturgy and life. He explores the 'indwelling of music, liturgy, and the Word,' providing specific examples and suggestions, reinforced by quotations from Pope Francis's *Desiderio Desideravi*, *Constitution on the Sacred Liturgy*, *Catechism of the Catholic Church*, and other documents, as seen through a lens of Dominican spirituality. Johnson poses questions and encourages readers to consider their own engagement with the Word 'for their betterment and for the greater holiness of the whole Church.'"

—Carol Browning, liturgical musician, composer, and member of
the Collegeville Composers Group

"*Incarnate in Word and Song* is like an afternoon coffee break with an observant and inquisitive friend. Drawing from fields as diverse as theology, literature, hymnody, and homiletics, Johnson brings his years of experience as a pastoral musician to bear on the relationship between preaching and liturgical music. Read it for fresh perspectives on preaching in the rich context of the liturgy."

> —Rhodora Beaton, Professor of Systematic Theology,
> Oblate School of Theology

"What can homilists learn from music ministers about preaching better? Quite a bit! The relationship between preaching the living Word in the midst of the assembly and singing that Word into life upon the lips of the faithful seems obvious but is rarely illuminated as deeply and clearly as Orin Johnson does in *Incarnate in Word and Song*. This book will inspire those who communicate the gospel in spoken word or ritual song to deepen their craft and work more closely together in leading the assembly to glorify God by their lives."

> —Diana Macalintal, Cofounder, TeamRCIA and Liturgy.life

"An expert in liturgical music and a gifted preacher himself, Orin Johnson explains how musical techniques from dynamics to poetry can help preachers craft more engaging homilies and reflections. Avoiding the trap of polemical arguments about liturgy, Johnson uses church guidance—especially Pope Francis's new document *Desiderio Desideravi*—to shed a refreshing light on the ultimate goal of both liturgical music and preaching, inspiring congregants to a more Christ-like life."

> —Colleen Dulle, *America Magazine*

"Orin Johnson's new work is an engaging exploration of the pastoral arts of preaching and liturgical music. Our tour guide, Johnson, is a master musician, composer, liturgist, and teacher who rarely lets his erudition show. He aptly resorts to humor, invites reader reflection, and, seamlessly, leads us to sincere spiritual reflection. *Incarnate in Word and Song: Exploring Music in Liturgy and Life is* recommended reading for preachers, musicians, liturgical ministers, and for every thoughtful lover of Catholic liturgy."

> —Peter Fisher Hesed, retired educator and director of music
> and liturgy

About the Cover

The cover art is a painting titled *O Magnum Mysterium* (O Great Mystery) by Minnesota artist Robyn Sand Anderson. The painting was inspired directly by Morten Lauridsen's famed choral setting of the Latin text from the Office of Matins on Christmas Day, which you can see below. This book explores the weaving and indwelling of music, liturgy, and The Word Made Flesh, as do the Matins text, Lauridsen's music, and Anderson's striking artwork.

To listen to *O Magnum Mysterium*, visit
    https://litpress.org/incarnate-word-song
For more on the artist, visit https://www.robynsandanderson.com/

O magnum mysterium, — O great mystery,
et admirabile sacramentum, — and wonderful sacrament,
ut animalia viderent — that animals should see
    Dominum natum, — the newborn Lord,
jacentem in praesepio! — lying in a manger!
Beata Virgo, cujus viscera — Blessed is the virgin whose womb
meruerunt portare — was worthy to bear
Dominum Iesum Christum. — the Lord, Jesus Christ.
Alleluia! — Alleluia!

To my parents, who first formed me in faith,
provided for years of organ and piano lessons,
and truly taught me how to live The Word.

"The true artist does not possess an art
but rather is possessed by it."
Pope Francis, *Desiderio Desideravi* (50)

Contents

Acknowledgments

Special thanks to:

Robyn Sand Anderson

Rhodora Beaton

David Brinker

Shannon Cerneka

Nathan Chase

Christian Cosas

Erin Hammond

John Kyler

Colleen Dulle, Tim Reidy, and *America* magazine

Fr. Raul Salas, OMI

Harold Velazquez

GIA, OCP, Hope Publishing, and ILP

Harvard University Press

Macmillan Publishers

Max Lucado

Fr. Bruno Esposito, OP, and Fr. Gregory Pearson, OP

Exploring the Relationship of Music, Liturgy, and The Word

The old joke goes something like this: A preacher, in the days of prohibition, was completing a sermon on temperance one Sunday morning and, with great expression, said, "Why, if I had all the beer in the world, I would take it and throw it into the river!" Then, with even greater emphasis, he continued, "And if I had all the wine in the world, I would take it and throw it into the river!" Finally, with all conviction and strength, he concluded, "And if I had all the whiskey in the world, I would take it and throw it into the river!" Taking a breath, the preacher then asked the choir to lead the congregation in the final hymn.

The music leader stood very cautiously and then announced, with a hint of a smile, "For our closing hymn today, let us sing hymn number 365: 'Shall We Gather at the River.'"

The tale, of course, is almost certainly apocryphal, yet it illustrates perfectly a few of the primary reasons to pursue a project such as this one. It has been understood, and generally well-practiced, for some time in Catholic liturgy that both the preaching and liturgical music ought to work in tandem with the other elements of any given liturgical celebration that are already prescribed: principally, the scripture and, to a lesser extent, the prayers of the mass. Less attention, though, has been given to the ways that preaching and liturgical music can work in tandem, as well as to what preaching and preachers might be able to gain from a study of liturgical music and the relationship between the two.

There is a certain unique and helpful perspective that liturgical musicians can bring to such an endeavor. Frequently, those in music ministry are at multiple masses each weekend, often more than any individual preacher or congregant might be. This gives these musicians several opportunities to hear a certain homily, to notice its structure, its delivery, its reception, and what makes any of those facets either work or not work. Oftentimes, a music minister will hear two or more preachers tackle the same scriptural material on a given Sunday and so have an opportunity few others have to compare and contrast the differing contents, deliveries, and receptions.

At a more foundational level, liturgical musicians can bring a particular and fruitful approach to knowledge and interpretation of scripture. The best music directors, after all, have spent years, if not decades, singing the words of sacred scripture as found in so much of our liturgical music, from the Propers and the Ordinary as found in the Missal to the contemporary music for liturgy written today. Beyond this, they also take great care, as mentioned above, to pair hymnody with the given scripture for a liturgy in ways that reiterate, enlighten, and offer new insights to the pericopes proclaimed in the midst of the assembly. From such a vantage point, liturgical music ministers could readily be seen as serving as preachers in their own certain way.

We also need not limit the preaching of The Word to liturgical examples, like at Eucharist or Liturgy of the Hours. What "The Word" is for us today goes beyond something scriptural; it is an Eternal Logos, alive and active still today, most fully manifest in Jesus Christ—and we, the faithful, are Christ's body, hands, and feet. We must be all things this Word is, and we must do all things this Word must do. We are love, hope, joy, and so much more; we must create, preach, evangelize, and so much more. As much as these manifestations of The Word happen in a sacred building, they must also move beyond the church doors, for in today's world that is perhaps where they are most needed: as a preaching of living The Word Incarnate such that those whom we encounter know exactly who our savior, our teacher, our brother, and our friend is.

But, of course, we need to know Christ first to preach him well. Consider the familiar admonition from William J. Toms: "You may be the only Bible some people read." Lest we be walking, talking empty books, blank pages, let us utilize instead every avenue to instill in the faithful a knowledge and love of Christ and a strong desire to serve him. Is this done only through words, however? No, says at least one significant voice from the early Church: "It is mainly the deeds of a love so noble that lead many to put a brand upon us. See how they love one another, they say, for they themselves are animated by mutual hatred; how they are ready even to die for one another, they say, for they themselves will sooner put to death" (Tertullian, *The Apology*, chap. 39). Who wouldn't want a church (and a Church) full of that kind of visible, sacrificial love?

Inspiring all of God's faithful to live that love ought to begin with the model set by the celebrant at liturgy. Pope Francis, in his apostolic letter *Desiderio Desideravi*,[1] tells us:

> In visiting Christian communities, I have noticed that their way of living the liturgical celebration is conditioned—for better or, unfortunately, for worse—by the way in which their pastor presides in the assembly. We could say that there are different "models" of presiding. Here is a possible list of approaches, which even though opposed to each other, characterize a way of presiding that is certainly inadequate: rigid austerity or an exasperating creativity, a spiritualizing mysticism or a practical functionalism, a rushed briskness or an overemphasized slowness, a sloppy carelessness or an excessive finickiness, a superabundant friendliness or priestly impassibility. Granted the wide range of these examples, I think that the inadequacy of these models of presiding have

> a common root: a heightened personalism of the celebrating
> style which at times expresses a poorly concealed mania to
> be the centre of attention. (54)

Indeed, preaching as part of the presider's ministry at liturgy must be an example for how the faithful are—and are not—to live their everyday lives, preaching The Word through deeds and interactions.

Having been a liturgical musician in diverse and disparate circumstances for more than thirty years now, there is a certain breadth of experience—along with more formal education—I am able to bring to this topic. Not only am I an accompanist, director, and singer, but I am also a composer of liturgical music as well as someone frequently called upon to reflect via spoken and written word on sacred scripture and the mysteries of our faith in front of God's holy people. I have been keenly aware that, at Eucharist, music and preaching are not disconnected from one another but indeed share a certain purpose and goal: to bring the faithful ever more deeply into the facets of the paschal mystery that the liturgy puts before us each time we gather, and to inspire them to live that faith with understanding and zeal outside the doors of the church. With that goal in mind, it makes sense to wonder how the two can work together and what insights into The Word—and living The Word—we might learn from a close study of the interrelationship of scripture, liturgy, and liturgical music.

This, then, will be a comprehensive look at various types of liturgical music along with their forms and structure, their language, their uses, and their implementations, placed in parallel with sacred scripture and liturgical elements. We will explore the relationship between the three and offer deeper explorations into the reasons to even take on such a project in the first place. We will dissect musical examples, and, on a practical level, offer illustrations of what liturgical preaching and real-life preaching moments might be like utilizing insights gained from such a study. And don't worry, reader, if you don't deem yourself especially musical! I promise there will not be too much jargon or "shop talk." Everything described and compared within this book ought to make sense to any lover of music, whether or not you yourself are musically talented or educated.

Our liturgies succeed, of course, by God's grace, no matter how well prepared (or not) they are, no matter how well (or not) they are celebrated, no matter how engaged (or not) an assembly is. There can be no denying, though, that they are most powerful with thoughtful preparation, careful execution, and absolute dedication to drawing in the assembly as fully as possible. Our evangelization efforts are most successful when they are relational, when we show to one another the same love, care, and devotion that Christ shows to us. To such ends, I offer this resource, which I pray is found helpful by preachers, evangelizers, lovers of scripture, and liturgical musicians alike.

1

Why Explore the Relationship between Music, Liturgy, and The Word

Theological Considerations

Before beginning in earnest, a thought experiment may suffice for giving you a personal reason for continuing on this journey with me. For a moment, I invite you to call to mind an instance of exceptional preaching you have heard, experienced. Place yourself, in your mind's eye, back into that context, calling to mind as many vivid details as you can. What was the place—a church or chapel, perhaps a funeral home or a gravesite, a hotel ballroom or your living room? Who was gathered there? When was it? What was going on in the world, your country, your town, or even your neighborhood? What was going on in your family, in your life specifically at that moment?

Now, bring to mind the service in which the preaching took place. What sort of prayer was it: mass, Liturgy of the Hours, a wake, or some other sort of prayer? What scripture or other texts was this preaching breaking open? What, if any, were the musical components of the service?

Lastly, call to mind the preacher specifically. What was, or is, their name? What did they look like while preaching? How were they dressed, vested? In your imagination, hear their voice again. How would you describe it? What unique attributes of their voice come to mind? And now think of the preaching itself. Was it delivered engagingly? What was it about the content or structure of those words that made them so memorable?

When I answer these questions, I recall a homily offered at a novena mass many years ago. The focus of that night of prayer was "Healing Within Family Relationships." In many other years, homilists at this novena had seemed to have the understanding that more words invariably made for a better homily, and so their homilies had often stretched to twenty or thirty minutes or beyond. But not this particular night, not this particular preacher.

To be honest, I don't even recall which scripture passages were proclaimed and attentively listened to that night, nor do I recall who the music ministers were or what was sung, even though I was, in my role as coordinator of music and liturgy at this particular national shrine, responsible for organizing both. What I do recall was that this priest, after proclaiming the gospel passage, returned to the presider's chair to retrieve a large, aqua-hued Tupperware bowl and lid. He had processed in with it, visibly, at the beginning of the mass but had until that point left it unexplained.

Holding it, he briefly detailed a family fight that followed a contentious Yahtzee game one night. The fight was not really about the game, of course. The game was just the spark that set off argument after argument about troubles and divisions from days, months, and even years in the past. Distresses and disagreements that had never been adequately dealt with were brought to the fore—and were not being dealt with positively on that night either.

He explained that it was like, as we've all experienced, leftovers which get put into large, aqua-hued Tupperware bowls and placed into the fridge—and then, often, neglected. The bowl remains in the fridge, shifting locations, then eventually moving to the back and being completely forgotten. Until.

Until, one day, months down the road, it is time to clean out the fridge, and the bowl and its contents are rediscovered. No one wants to open that lid and deal with whatever has become of the contents inside. But it, of course, must be done by someone, sometime, somehow. Would it not have been easier to have taken care of things at the very beginning, before the contents of the bowl had been given a chance to spoil, mold over, and become much more unpleasant and difficult to deal with? And after taking a brief pause, he concluded, "Don't put your family troubles into a Tupperware bowl."

And then the preacher sat down and, by example, invited all to a moment of silent reflection. He spoke for, as I recall, 7 minutes that night. And of the roughly 120 novena homilies I heard over my tenure at that shrine, this is the only one I remember in such detail. No one needed 2 or 3 times the number of words to understand exactly what the homily was trying to impart, even though it was brief, didn't directly interact with the scripture, and dwelled nearly exclusively on the level of analogy and metaphor.

There were many details that made this particular preaching example so effective that night, not the least of which was obvious advance preparation. Shorter homilies, any shorter texts, often take twice as long to prepare than much longer ones. In terms of delivery, it was not flashy or attention grabbing per se, but it did dwell in a familiar world of Yahtzee games and Tupperware bowls. The content was nothing novel, nor were its insights innovative, but that same content allowed the receivers of it to enter into the metaphoric world he created, to place themselves and their own lives into the preaching, almost as if in quiet dialogue. And lastly, the homily ended with a memorable "hook," a short phrase that would reverberate in everyone's hearts and minds for the rest of the evening and far beyond it—for me, it is still doing so some fifteen and more years later.

It might not be immediately obvious, but some of the liturgical preaching techniques this preacher used to grab my attention— structure, familiarity, catchy language, and more—are also found in the world of music and, in particular, within liturgical music. No matter what one's particular preference is in terms of musical styles, both inside and outside of the church doors, there are some elements we can name and describe that make any music more powerful, more engaging, and more impactful. While there are many kinds of liturgical music, there are similar aspects in common across all liturgical pieces that help them achieve their goals—aspects that can be both named and described.

Music, too, can help us gain insights into The Word, both sacred scripture (the written word) and Jesus Christ (the Eternal Logos). Musical compositional attributes like melody, harmony, and rhythm, alongside performance attributes like tempo and volume, provide each of us a lens with which we can bring The Word into greater focus, and they can even show us new inroads to new understandings. In turn, these insights can make the same Christ more obviously present in both liturgical preaching and our daily lives.

But, before we get too far ahead of ourselves, why ought we explore this particular and distinctive relationship between music, liturgy, and The Word at all? Why not, for instance, explore the relationship between liturgical art and preaching, or between sacred architecture and the gospels? Truth be told, someone should! I am certain there is value to be found in such research and writing, but I am not the one to talk about such things intelligently. However, my particular upbringing, education, and experience do allow me, I believe, to embark on this particular exploration and to do so fruitfully.

Further, there are already connections between music, liturgy, and The Word found explicitly in our scripture, tradition, and within the liturgy itself, as reformed at the Second Vatican Council. This interconnectedness is a key reason to embark on this journey—but it really is more than mere interconnectedness. Just as the three Persons of the Trinity are distinct yet one, dwelling within one another, forming an intimate community in which one Person of the Trinity penetrates the others and is penetrated by them, these facets of our church life can be seen and explored in the same manner.

So, by grafting such perichoresis onto a study of music, liturgy, and The Word, we find both theological and spiritual reasons to forge ahead. There are practical, "boots on the ground" reasons for this study too, and some of those reasons are quite urgent indeed. But we shall wait to point them out until the end of our journey, that they might better propel us more firmly into action, into revitalized efforts to help build God's reign.

For now, let us take a moment to briefly look at this foundational indwelling of music, liturgy, and The Word, upon which we can then build further advantageous connections and relationships between the three.

2

Music, Liturgy, and The Word

Connections in Sacred Scripture

There are countless instances of music playing an integral role in the lives of the faithful throughout both Christian and Hebrew Scriptures. We can likely name several without needing even a moment to think. Luke is known as the Gospel of Songs, for it includes the Gloria sung by the angels at Christ's birth as well as the canticles of Mary, Zechariah, and Simeon. He again writes in Acts 16:25 that Paul and Silas were praying and singing hymns in prison while the other captives listened to them, the music here serving as evangelization and likely even catechesis for the others. This example, you might realize already, has a particular relevance for this study.

The gospels contain at least one instance of Jesus and his followers including music in their religious practices: they sing a hymn following Jesus's last supper (Mark 14:26; Matt 26:30) before journeying to the Mount of Olives, where Jesus is betrayed.

The epistles contain several references to music and its value to the faithful. In Colossians 3:16, Paul instructs his readers, "Let the word of Christ dwell in you richly, as in all wisdom you teach and admonish one another, singing psalms, hymns, and spiritual songs with gratitude in your hearts to God." Here we see that the music is directly linked to teaching and admonishing, elements that are, for better or worse, often found in preaching—both within church buildings and outside of them. Paul also offers a similar instruction to the Ephesians (5:19-20), while the epistle of James (5:13) invites singing praise when one is able, "in good spirits."

The book of Revelation is also full of music and singing. Angels around the throne cry "Holy, holy, holy" (4:8; see also Isa 6:3), and then, in Revelation 14:2-3, we read,

> I heard a sound from heaven like the sound of rushing water or a loud peal of thunder. The sound I heard was like that of harpists playing their harps. They were singing [what seemed to be] a new hymn before the throne, before the four living creatures and the elders. No one could learn this hymn except the hundred and forty-four thousand who had been ransomed from the earth.

Here, "a new hymn" is being created, both spatially within and symbolic of the new Jerusalem, by the Christian people who have survived the time of trial.

In the Old Testament, we of course must first recall the psalms, which have been for thousands of years a musical expression of faith—first for the Jewish people, and today for Christians as well. In these 150 texts we find the full range of human emotion: joy, sadness, doubt, confidence, lament, praise, thanksgiving, and more. These passions are embedded in our relationship with the divine, and the psalms not only encompass them, not only express them, but also help us to connect with and musically converse with our Creator and the whole of the Christian community.

In addition to the psalms, we easily find other music elsewhere in the Old Testament: the Song of Songs, the women singing when David defeated Goliath, and Isaiah's lament over the worthless vineyard, to name but a few.

The final examples I will include here are found in Exodus 15: the hymns sung by the Israelites who have just crossed the Red Sea into freedom. Part of their first hymn, the *Mi Chamocha* (Who Is Like You?), is part of Jewish ritual prayers to this day—understandably so! This is the quintessential song of freedom from captivity, a freedom celebrated every Passover. And this same canticle is one of the few specifically prescribed pieces of music in our Catholic Missal, attached to the Exodus 15 pericope that must be included at the Easter Vigil mass every year. This pivotal moment in our ancestors' journey of faith is very nearly liturgical on its own and, as such, is part of our faith journey to this day; our baptism is, anamnetically, this same crossing through the sea into freedom—how could we not, then, sing a hymn of praise as well? We shall see later in this book how this Exodus moment is part of a rather clear and obvious example of liturgical anamnesis: the blessing of baptismal water.

Music, especially singing, is an inseparable part of being a person of faith. Scripture shows us this over and over again. It is fitting and necessary that we allow music to inform every aspect of our faith lives, including our knowledge and understanding of the divine, our acts of worship, and the sharing of The Word we offer to one another on our journey to holiness. "Ignorance of scripture is ignorance of Christ," declared St. Jerome, which is at once both challenging and compelling. He who may be most responsible for bringing the word of God to all the faithful is speaking here not of any academic formation or literary scholarship but simply of one's ability and even desire to meet and enter into the word of God—both the written word and the Eternal Logos—and to do so deeply. Ultimately, the two are one and the same—two different expressions, to be sure, yet of the one Christ. To know and become one with Christ, one must know and become one with scripture. It is those same texts that show us that our faith is inextricably linked to music and song. To complete the circle, it is so often music and song that help us to know, love, and serve scripture—to know, love, and serve God, whose Son, Christ, is the fullness of God's revelation. Therefore, scripture must be shared, broken open, understood, and, ultimately, lived accordingly.

3

Music, Liturgy, and The Word

Connections in Christian Tradition

We know, too, that music played an important role in the worship, theology, and evangelization efforts of the early Church (and the Church of the next two thousand years as well). I offer but a few examples here, which were picked for their particular consequence to this project, to help us draw some important foundational connections between music, liturgy, and The Word. There are, of course, many other examples.

Pliny the Younger (61–113) wrote to the emperor Trajan describing the Christian practice of gathering before sunrise and repeating antiphonally "a hymn to Christ, as to God." The relevance here I wish to draw attention to is more than the recognition that Christ was (and is) divine. I note more so that, in this act of worship, the music described was apparently performed liturgically and with an antiphonal structure—a relational back-and-forth between members of the faithful assembled in prayer. Presumably, such an antiphonal form ought to be seen as dialogical in nature, the faithful in a sort of scripted, forced conversation with one another—and we shall hear more later about how these sorts of forced conversations are still very much a part of our liturgical practices today and how they could be a valuable tool in knowing and sharing The Word as well. Such liturgical interaction and "dialogue" among the faithful, one could argue, promotes love and unity within the community of believers or, if not, at least encourages communal participation and engagement.

Clement of Alexandria (c. 150–c. 215) linked the music Christians created to the Divine Creator directly, saying, "The *musica humana* was created in the image of God, and is the crown of all the *musica mundana*." Greek musical cosmology taught that the harmonies of the universe (*musica mundana*) ranked just above the harmonies of humankind (*musica humana*), but Clement here is promoting unity between the faithful and God by placing our music at the pinnacle of all music in the universe. Just as Adam and Eve are described in the creation stories of Genesis, human music is itself in the image and likeness of God. Notably, Clement was concerned with distinguishing music created by humans directly (internally)—that is, singing—from instrumental music, created in a sense outside the human body (externally), which he saw as "superfluous music, which enervates men's souls."

Though some might find fruitful ways to quibble about that distinction, Clement, even if without specific purpose, noted that musical connection to God pertained to music emanating from within human beings, not outside of them. The human voice is, ultimately, the only musical instrument that is within a human person and is capable of expressing tangible and specific texts. The relationship and unity we have with the divine, for Clement, is found truly and only in human music—that is, singing, with words and melodies themselves being also in the image and likeness of God.

God uses the first-person plural when creating humans in Genesis: "Let us make human beings in our image" (1:26). Many theologians find dense meaning within this brief clause. To them, it shows that the Trinity was present at creation and that each Person was involved in the creative act, that God is eternally relational, and so humans, created in God's image, are also created to be relational beings. Our evangelization ought to strive for a similar relationship with those around us, who should also be seen as formed in the image and likeness of God. In short, our preaching, our sharing The Word, must be relational to be what it needs to be and to do what the Church needs it to do.

While the next attribution is dubious, let us take a moment to explore St. Augustine's maxim, "The one who sings well prays twice." It has long been known that one practical aspect of singing well is audible projection, the art of giving one's voice a strength of volume and fullness of tone, and that by these attributes, the songs created, their melodies and words, carry further and more intelligibly than normal speech does. This is in part why there are ancient traditions of our liturgy being so musical. In large worship spaces, in days long before microphones, amplifiers, and booming speakers, singing the words of our faith allowed them to better fill a large gothic church, for instance, and be more readily heard and understood throughout.

The amplification that Augustine's maxim brings to our attention is not sonic, though, but spiritual. And while Augustine intimates that the spiritual amplification is additive, I much prefer to think of it as multiplicative. It seems odd—if not outright unreasonable—to place some sort of numerical value on either prayer or music, but to illustrate the point, suppose one could say that the value of a certain prayer is three units—whatever those units are—and that the value of a bit of music is also three units. To me, if that prayer and that bit of music are combined, the result isn't additive (that is, the combined value doesn't become six units) but rather is multiplicative (it becomes nine units). It's the faith version of "The whole is greater than the sum of its parts."

Perhaps a real-world example will explain this better. Place yourself for a moment in a scene where, on your birthday, you are arriving back home after staying late at work. Oddly, the lights are out as you approach the front door, but you are a bit too tired to have any suspicion as to why. As you open the door and step foot into your living room, suddenly all the lights come on at once, and your spouse and other family members and friends pop out from behind the couch and the table. Then, as one, they joyously fulfill the surprise birthday party ritual by producing a cake adorned with more candles than you would like to admit and joyously *reciting* with one another,

> Happy birthday to you.
> Happy birthday to you.
> Happy birthday, dear Suzy,
> Happy birthday to you.

Now, imagine precisely the same scenario, except at the appropriate time your gathered family and friends fulfill the party's expectation by merely humming the familiar tune that goes with these lyrics, without the words themselves. One without the other has some semblance of meaning and purpose, but the two combined, the words with the tune, have a meaning that is more than the sum of the two parts together.

By now, perhaps, you are saying back to me, through the ether, "This is all well and good, but I know someone who doesn't sing well at all!" You may even be saying that about yourself. What about that person who doesn't sing well? Are they also capable of "praying twice"? Through the ether I say back to you: The judgment that one doesn't sing well is almost always in error. More typically, that person simply has not had experience or education in singing, in using the musical instrument that resides within themself. Certainly, at the very least, it is true that any one of us can sing as well as we can, whatever skill level that may be.

There are, though, a few folks out there who truly cannot sing very well. My father, Orville, was one of them. He grew up during the Great Depression, and while he wanted to take music lessons, acquiring an instrument and paying for instruction just wasn't an option for his family then. So, later in life, he could vocally produce about three different bass pitches, almost always off key and only when prodded. Usually, I was the one prodding him, most often during mass—he was often silent during the singing otherwise. He knew enough about reading music to know that if the dots or circles were higher up on the staff, then he should pick one of the higher of his three notes, and if they were toward the bottom, he should pick his lower notes.

What my father was doing, when he did sing in church, was, in the words of Psalm 66 (and other psalms), making "a joyful noise unto God" (King James Version). Said another way, God had given my father the gift of this particular vocal instrument, and (when prodded) he was giving the gift right back to God—which is, in broad strokes, an important facet of our eucharistic celebrations, is it not? We return to God gifts of bread and wine, produced by us from the gifts of wheat and grapes God gave to us. At Eucharist, we truly return our very selves as gift and sacrifice to God. Dad was giving back the best that he could, which is all that God desires; in doing so, I can say with certitude that Dad, too, was "praying twice." So should we all!

In the same way, our preaching, our evangelizing, and our sharing and living of The Word should be the very best we have to offer. Is our preaching, for instance, one that is well educated and spiritually molded? Do we see each opportunity to preach as an opportunity to craft our words and their delivery better than we did the last time? In our day-to-day lives, no matter our formation and experience, do we strive to do the best we can in every instance and give the gift of that opportunity and our very selves to one another (and, by doing so, give ourselves as sacrifice back to God)? In all these things, does our knowledge of and sharing of The Word lead people to live their faith in a way that amplifies their belief? Does it lead them to prayer? Or are your words and deeds, on at least one level, prayer themselves?

We are just now beginning to see the pervasive and meaningful connections between the musical arts, liturgical praxis, and The Word. We are just beginning to observe that the relationship these three important components of our faith have is both scriptural and part of our tradition. It makes complete sense, then, that both music and sharing of The Word are foundational to our liturgical practices, both historically and today. But within the liturgy, music and preaching should do more than just reside near each other;

they must enter into relationship with one other and make each other better. Indeed, they must amplify one another, learn from one another, and help one another to grow and blossom—all to enter into meaningful relationship with our ordered prayer.

4

Music, Liturgy, and The Word

Connections in the Liturgy Itself

Beyond just "sharing space," liturgical music and effective preaching are inextricably linked by virtue of what our liturgical documents tell us liturgy is. Foundational among these documents is, of course, *Sacrosanctum Concilium*, the Constitution on the Sacred Liturgy (CSL), the first document promulgated by Vatican II in late 1963. If, perhaps, you are not already familiar with that text, let me suggest placing a bookmark here and pausing to become so! (The text and various commentaries are easily found online these days.) For this project, I will bring to our attention only a few key passages from CSL that, after having been studied, digested, and lived, have truly become beacons that guide liturgical practices in our Church to this day.

Perhaps the foremost of these beacons is the document's call to "full, conscious, and active" participation, found in the following two paragraphs and several other places:

> It is very much the wish of the church that all the faithful
> should be led to take that full, conscious, and active part in
> liturgical celebrations which is demanded by the very nature
> of the liturgy, and to which the Christian people, "a chosen
> race, a royal priesthood, a holy nation, a redeemed people"
> (1 Pet 2:9, 4-5) have a right and to which they are bound by
> reason of their Baptism. (CSL 14)

> To develop active participation, the people should be encour-
> aged to take part by means of acclamations, responses, psalms,
> antiphons, hymns, as well as by actions, gestures and bodily
> attitudes. And at the proper time a reverent silence should be
> observed. (CSL 30)

We must spend some time here breaking open just why "full, conscious, and active" participation is so important to our liturgy and our faith. The Church's liturgy, CSL tells us, is the paramount tangible relationship between the divine and the faithful: "Christ, indeed, always associates the church with himself in this great work in which God is perfectly glorified and men and women are sanctified" (CSL 7). St. Ignatius and, more broadly, Jesuit spirituality in fact extend this paradigm to the whole of Christian life: *Ad Majorem Dei Gloriam*, "For the greater glory of God." Pair this with the Ignatian spirituality of "seeking God in everything," and one quickly sees that liturgy is not just a mirror of life and not just a part of it; it *is* life, and life, too, *is* liturgy. If we accept that the liturgy is so relational and so necessary for our lives, our sanctification and salvation, then CSL's promotion of our complete presence, awareness, and participation at liturgy—and life!—should come as no surprise.

This is what it means to be baptized, after all: we are members of Christ's Body, members of one another, one Church and one Body (see *Catechism of the Catholic Church* 1267). We share in the priestly mission of Christ and in the common priesthood of all believers (*Catechism* 1269). More explicitly, "Incorporated into the Church by Baptism, the faithful have received the sacramental character that consecrates them for Christian religious worship. The baptismal seal enables and commits Christians to serve God by a vital participation in the holy liturgy of the Church and to exercise their baptismal priesthood by the witness of holy lives and practical charity" (*Catechism* 1273).

Perhaps it is because of these reasons and more that the rite of baptism is especially imbued with scripture and anamnesis.

Mass is full of scripture, and the newest English translation has made that even more apparent. "Lord, I am not worthy / that you should enter under my roof" is but one example. It draws a direct connection from Eucharist to the centurion's profession of faith in Matthew 8:8. Other sacraments, too, are full of scripture hiding in plain sight: congregational acclamations used at baptism and matrimony, for instance, are drawn directly from scripture.

Of course, it is in the mass where we encounter the Christian anamnesis par excellence: the presencing of the Lord by the great prayer of thanksgiving and the words of institution. This presencing is not passive, nor is it one of mere memory. We are actively realizing anew and entering into the paschal mystery—past, present, and future. We should also be careful to note that we ought not confuse anamnesis with a sort of allegorical interpretation of our liturgical rites—for instance, in the manner that some medieval theologians likened the various parts of the mass, by the use of foreshadowing known sometimes as "type" and "antitype," directly to various parts of Christ's Passion. No, anamnesis is much more profound, more imbued with mystery and presence.

Outside of Eucharist, we may find several instances of anamnesis in the rites of baptism. The person to be baptized is to be greeted at the church doors, a reminder that Jesus himself is the gate of salvation. (Some church doors bear the Latin inscription *Domus Dei et Porta Coeli*, "House of God and Gate of Heaven.") In the moment the person is given their baptismal name, we are reminded of all those in scripture who were given a new name to symbolize their new, faith-filled purpose—indeed, their very consecration. The scriptures prescribed for baptisms outside of mass are perhaps the most obvious anamnetic tool, most fully realized with effective and relevant preaching. If included as part of the baptismal rite, the Litany of the Saints makes present to those assembled the Church of history and the Church already united with God in heaven.

The blessing of the water of baptism is a *tour de force* memorial of aquatic salvation history. Prior to the words of blessing themselves, great moments of God's breaking into our lives are recalled; the creation narrative, Noah and the Flood, the exodus through the sea, Jesus's baptism, the blood and water that flowed from Jesus's side at the crucifixion, and the disciples being sent to baptize are all memorialized. By these moments and the imagery proper to baptism—the candle, the white garment, the chrismation, and even immersion, when possible, that dying and rising embodied ritually—we come to understand that at Vatican II baptism was reoriented to call the faithful to their rights and obligations as members of the Christian community. The entire life of the faithful proceeds from baptism, sustained by the Eucharist and the other sacraments. It's not only about washing away the stain of original sin; it's so much more.

In short, by baptism we are no longer disengaged, passive, unaware. No, we are fully, consciously, and actively Christian. We are fully, consciously, and actively in relationship with God and the divine mission of salvation. With liturgy standing as the paramount tangible expression of that relationship, let us turn our attention back to its fullest and most expressive manifestations, especially its facets of liturgical music and preaching.

Catholic liturgy, as already mentioned, does not merely include some singing from time to time; rather, Catholic liturgy is a sung liturgy. The list of what is sung, at a minimum, is listed for us above in the quote from CSL 30. Further, the expectation is that there is congregational participation in all of the types of singing mentioned. Silence is also an important part of our liturgies, as well as of liturgical music and preaching, and we shall devote more time to silence and its implications later on. Let us note here, too, that few parishes in actuality do sung liturgy well, or at least as fully as they could, and we'll dive into that a little more deeply later on as well. The key element to notice for now is that congregational liturgical participation is expected and that the participation should be "real" and, in fact, is only made "real" if it is external, if it is active.

There has been much liquid and digital ink spilled in recent years over the translation of the Latin *actuoso* here—"actual" versus "active"—and how an assembly's participation in the liturgy may take both internal and external forms. This is true, generally speaking. It is difficult, though, to successfully maintain a stance that the assembly's participation in the liturgy is not at least sometimes necessarily external and active when viewing these passages from CSL; the whole of CSL, and the Vatican II documents that followed, explain, clarify, and expand upon just the opposite. In short, my stance is that active participation, at least when it comes to singing, must be external—creating rather than merely listening—most of the time. It's akin to the familiar passage in the book of James:

> Indeed someone may say, "You have faith and I have works." Demonstrate your faith to me without works, and I will demonstrate my faith to you from my works. (2:18)

Allow me, please, to offer my own alteration:

> Demonstrate to me your active participation without external signs, and I will demonstrate to you my active participation by them.

All of this leads us here: the structures of liturgy and its individual components should be, to borrow a musical term, *resonant* with one another. If the call to active participation is true, and true in this particular way for the music, then it should be so throughout the liturgy and through each portion and component similarly. When this really and truly happens, the whole of the liturgy—including preaching—becomes written on our hearts more indelibly, and the fruits of the liturgy grow abundantly and become that much more apparent. If we are called to live our faith in ways that people can obviously see and tangibly experience, should not the whole of liturgy model this too?

I recall a particular adaptation introduced to the liturgy a few decades ago, especially prevalent among youth ministry efforts in the United States: a reworking of the dismissal dialogue. It gave the assembly this text to conclude mass: "The mass never ends! It must be lived! So let us go forth to love and serve the Lord!" The goal of this change, as I understood the pastoral reasoning behind it, was rather like the goal of this book: to unify the relationship shared between liturgical music, liturgy, and The Word such that one's knowledge and love of Christ could be effectively shared in every moment of liturgy and life.

For the purposes of this book, The Word, we have already noted, is both sacred scripture and the Eternal Logos—The Word that God uttered at creation, who eventually broke into human time and space as Jesus, the Christ, and who now sits at the right hand of the Father. Liturgy, again for our purposes here, is the formal, corporate, prescribed moments of prayer given to us by the Church, notably excluding devotional prayers like Stations of the Cross or the rosary. We have not yet had a chance to define more exactly what is meant here by liturgical music or by sharing The Word, via preaching specifically or by our lives; we will arrive at these moments soon enough. For now, a glimpse ahead at some of the benefits of exploring and implementing such a study of the relationship of these elements will have to suffice.

I challenge you, right this moment, to recite aloud as much of Psalm 91 as you can. Go ahead, right this moment. Perhaps a few of you can, but for most people, even people of great faith, such a request typically yields mostly silence. Yet, like it or leave it, almost any of us could sing a verse or two—or all—of "On Eagle's Wings" by Fr. Michael Joncas, which is, you have probably guessed, a setting of Psalm 91 in paraphrase. In this way, music has an almost unimaginable power: to place on our hearts and our lived experiences some profound words of scripture; music here instantly creates relationship among itself, liturgy, and The Word. The rising, sequential refrain, easy to learn and evocative of an eagle taking flight and rising to the heavens, is in some ways what musicians call a "hook," a little snippet of melody, rhythm, and harmony, memorable and catchy, a feature of many popular and unforgettable pieces of music, be they secular or sacred. How we might long for our liturgical preaching to also have such a hook—like there was in that novena homily I recalled in chapter one—for the faithful to retain and truly put into practice, to live! Ought we not, for example, explore the possible ways to add such a technique to our preaching toolkits, to be able to inscribe the homily on the hearts of the faithful in the way that music is able to more innately?

The task before us is this: to more deeply and with clear intent explore the relationship between liturgical music, liturgy, and The Word, for the betterment of our liturgical celebrations, for the betterment of the Christian community. The liturgy, after all, is "the summit toward which the activity of the church is directed; it is also the source from which all its power flows. For the goal of apostolic endeavor is that all who are made children of God by faith and Baptism should come together to praise God in the midst of his church, to take part in the sacrifice and to eat the Lord's Supper" (CSL 10). We remind ourselves, too, that "Christ, indeed, always associates the church with himself in this great work in which God is perfectly glorified and men and women are sanctified. The church is his beloved bride who calls to its Lord, and through him offers worship to the eternal Father" (CSL 7).

5

What Is Liturgical Music?

To properly begin our exploration in earnest, it will help us to define some terms. When it comes to liturgical music, this is an especially important task. It is frequently the case that music ministers have a very particular notion unto themselves as to what is and is not "legitimate" liturgical music, or at least they have very strong preferences for certain styles, instrumentation, languages, etc. For the purpose of this project, these attributes are not especially important. What is important is that high-quality liturgical music (and terrible liturgical music, for that matter) arises throughout Christian history and from as many places and cultures as there ever have been or ever will be. For the present project of linking together liturgical music, liturgy, and The Word, characteristics like style or instrumentation ultimately don't matter very much. We will be spending more of our time considering liturgical descriptions and categorizations of music as well as elements of melody, harmony, rhythm, structure, and expression that many types of liturgical music—and music in general—share in common.

So, for this study, the categories of liturgical music that are most useful are the ones that were mentioned in the previous chapter when quoting from CSL 30: acclamations, responses, psalmody, antiphons, and songs. As the years have passed since CSL was promulgated, other documents have further elaborated that this listing of liturgical music was (and is) presented hierarchically, in order of use and importance. Most recently, the 2007 document *Sing to the Lord* (STTL) from the United States Conference of Catholic Bishops used this listing of liturgical music wedded to the principle of "progressive solemnity" (see STTL 110). STTL did not introduce this concept—it was found previously in the General Instruction of the Liturgy of the Hours as well as in Vatican II's *Musicam Sacram* (Instruction on Music in the Liturgy). Earlier, I stated that few parishes do sung liturgy well, and this concept of progressive solemnity is what informs that opinion. The idea here is that the first thing to be sung, at the least solemn sort of celebrations, are the acclamations, the first in the list CSL gave us. Then, at the next level of solemnity, one would add responses, then psalmody, then antiphons, and, finally, songs. Many parishes I know flip that musical hierarchy completely on its head, upside down, in terms of common practice.

I describe progressive solemnity not because this project is about it per se but because I want to highlight that the definition of liturgical music being used here may be more expansive than expected. To attend to each of these various categories of liturgical music and implement them in practice is to more fully sing the liturgy as expected by CSL and place the liturgy more fully, more consciously, and more actively on the hearts of the faithful. There are aspects of each of these categories to which the goal of knowing, sharing, and living The Word can connect and from which it can learn and better itself.

First on the hierarchy of the assembly's musical participation at liturgy are acclamations. These are, generally speaking, brief outbursts of praise and assent. The most familiar of these are the two most important acclamations of the Catholic mass: the Alleluia and the Amen. The Alleluia is the faithful's hymn of praise, an acclamation that greets the words and deeds of Christ (the gospels) about to be proclaimed in our midst. The Amen is the congregation's assent to the whole of the eucharistic prayer, prayed together as the Body of Christ with the priest-celebrant as the head, *in persona Christi Capitis*. These two congregational moments are the pinnacles of the mass and therefore require acclamations that are pinnacles of the active participation of the assembly. There are, however, other liturgical acclamations: the memorial acclamation immediately following the words of consecration and the "Blessed be God for ever" at the offertory, to name two.

Next, following the order of progressive solemnity, are responses, sometimes known as dialogues because they are in fact a rather stilted, scripted moment of dialogue between celebrant (or other liturgical minister) and assembly. The responses the liturgy gives the assembly within Eucharist include "Thanks be to God" following the readings, "And with your spirit" following an ordained minister's "The Lord be with you," and the whole of the preface dialogue, adding in "We lift them up to the Lord" and "It is right and just." Perhaps the preface dialogue is sung in your local parish, but it is rather infrequent to hear the dialogues during the Liturgy of the Word ever sung!

When our liturgical documents mention psalmody, we of course think of the responsorial psalm at mass. CSL and STTL are not exclusively about mass, though, and the Church utilizes several other liturgies in its corporate worship. The Liturgy of the Hours is built on singing through all 150 psalms (and other scriptural canticles) in their fullness, for instance. And even at mass, one can find psalms permeating the liturgy beyond just the one moment during the Liturgy of the Word. The most frequent place one might find them outside the responsorial psalm is in the proper antiphons prescribed for each celebration.

The proper antiphons assigned to each Eucharist are lately gaining more use as liturgists and music directors appreciate them as prescribed parts of the liturgy (found explicitly in the Missal) and for their scriptural content. In some ways, scripture does not saturate the liturgy and our very lives the way it ought to; use of the entrance and communion antiphons is one way to address that deficiency. Very often, these antiphons are psalm verses themselves or are at least scriptural. Even if the antiphon itself is not from a psalm, the antiphons in practice are meant to be paired with a corresponding psalm text, with the antiphon itself reappearing every so often as the psalm is sung, or at least at the beginning and end. As music meant to accompany processions, a single musical phrase (the antiphon standing alone) is infrequently, if ever, enough to fully accompany such a liturgical action. Some of us will recall days not long ago when refrains of hymns were at least sometimes called antiphons; these proper antiphons for each liturgical celebration can and should be used in such a way, if one deems the antiphons fruitful for the worship of the local community.

The last of the liturgical music mentioned by CSL and STTL are songs: hymns and canticles—both those ancient ones prescribed by the Missal and those newly composed. By being mentioned last hierarchically, this sort of music is, in theory, reserved for the most solemn of liturgical celebrations, yet in practice this is often the only music utilized at some of our simpler masses (instead of beginning with sung acclamations and sung responses, as progressive solemnity desires). This category of music, songs, includes the familiar melodies found in whichever hymnal that graces your pews. It also includes other familiar liturgical and scriptural hymns such as the Gloria at Eucharist; the canticles of Mary, Zechariah, and Simeon at the Liturgy of the Hours; other scriptural hymns like Paul's famous Christic canticle in his epistle to the Philippians ("that at the name of Jesus . . ."); or hymns from the Christian tradition like the "Pange Lingua Gloriosi," typically sung on Holy Thursday.

Acclamations, responses, psalmody, antiphons, and songs—these are the types of liturgical music, regardless of any other particular identifying traits they may have, that we will explore in the coming pages for anything they can offer in relationship with the liturgy and at the service of The Word. Each in turn will put before us various aspects of composition and techniques of delivery that can inform our efforts and sharing The Word in a more relevant and engaging way.

6

What Is Preaching?
What Is Sharing The Word?

Whereas liturgical music can be discussed categorically, it's not really possible to do so when it comes to liturgical preaching. Instead, we can describe opportunities where this preaching might occur: during the homily at mass, Liturgy of the Hours, other Liturgy of the Word services like a funeral vigil, other ritual prayers, devotional prayers, and even times outside of ordered prayer. To a large extent, though, no matter the opportunity, the preaching itself does not typically vary much from example to example, at least not in the way that examples from the various categories of liturgical music do. Think about the difference, for instance, between a one-word acclamation and a hymn lasting five minutes or more. While preaching can vary quite a lot in terms of length, content, preacher, receiver, and more, it is not helpful or even possible to try to categorize preaching in the same manner as liturgical music.

What is possible, especially for our purposes here, is to ponder and describe the function of liturgical preaching: why it exists and what it is meant to accomplish. Then we can also discuss the manners in which it goes about meeting those goals. We should first attend to these topics before bringing these purposes, goals, and methods into conversation with liturgical music. In this way, the elements of structures of the various types of music for worship can both inform preaching and form preachers.

"Preach the Gospel at all times; when necessary, use words," St. Francis supposedly taught. Is not our whole life a preaching of The Word? Well, yes, to answer the rhetorical question succinctly. We have already discussed how liturgy and life are interwoven, thoroughly connected. While we concern ourselves in this project with particular occasions of preaching as more typically imagined, these instances, too, can learn from the idea that one's whole life should be preaching without words—that one's way of living, in loving and relational sacrificial service to one another, should bring the scriptures to life in an engaging and relevant way. First, let us explore the breaking open of The Word in the liturgical context. Later, we can explore our daily living and sharing The Word outside of the church doors.

In Catholicism, the most frequent occurrence of preaching is the homily at mass. The word "homily" is derived from the Greek word *homilia*, which means "to have communion with" or "to communicate with." The preposition here is important—"with," not "to" or "at." The word *homilia* points toward something quite relational here, union sought through an exchange of ideas rather than speech that is merely transactional or listened to only in order to reply rather than to truly understand. Again, we see that each element of liturgy should be imbued with the foundational character of our Christian faith: relationship.

Returning to CSL, we find a couple of foundational insights into the homily and its function and purpose as well, once we tug at the threads enough. CSL 24 tells us that "Sacred scripture is of the greatest importance in the celebration of the liturgy. For from it are drawn the lessons which are read and which are explained in the homily." I suspect many of us have heard homilies that we would describe as "lessons," especially when the homilist comes to us from some sort of educational, academic background. Note that CSL here describes the scripture themselves as the lessons, which need only to be "explained" in the homily. So, if we are to believe that a homily ought not be an academic lecture—or anything remotely similar—what should it be?

Later in CSL, we are given more detail: "By means of the homily, the mysteries of the faith and the guiding principles of the christian life are expounded from the sacred text during the course of the liturgical year. The homily is strongly recommended since it forms part of the liturgy itself" (CSL 52). We should first realize that the use of "expounded" here is roughly equivalent to the use of the word "explained," which we just pondered. That is, to reiterate, the homily is not to be a lesson in and of itself but should instead deal relationally with bringing the paschal mystery (in its many facets) into conversation with the Christian life and the principles that guide each of us, individually and corporately, on that journey.

Should one turn to an internet search for answers, one of the first definitions returned for the word "homily" is "a religious discourse that is intended primarily for spiritual edification rather than doctrinal instruction; a sermon."[1] It goes without saying, hopefully, that the results of an internet search do not create binding liturgical law! It also goes without saying, at least for myself, that I'd prefer hearing many more homilies that deal with spiritual edification rather than with doctrinal instruction—and I suspect many of the faithful agree with me there. If we take "edification" to be synonymous with "uplift," then this definition of a homily falls into line with (or at least forms a pattern with) what we've seen from the CSL as well the etymology of the word "homily" itself. We can then begin a process of integration by which we could say that a homily's why, what, and how is to relationally uplift the faithful in their day-to-day living by explaining and applying the mysteries of the faith to real life here and now.

The 2015 Homiletic Directory from the Congregation for Divine Worship and the Discipline of the Sacraments agrees with all of this: the homily is not to be abstract, catechetical, or "purely moralistic, doctrinaire, or simply a lecture on biblical exegesis" (6). The homily is to be, it says, quoting the General Instruction of the Roman Missal (65), "an explanation of some aspect of the readings from Sacred Scripture or of another text from the Ordinary or the Proper of the Mass of the day and should take into account both the mystery being celebrated and the particular needs of the listeners" (quoted in 9). Further confirmation and expansion of these details and those in the previous paragraphs here may be found in the Introduction to the Lectionary, paragraph 24.

With a definition of purpose in hand—to relationally uplift the faithful in their day-to-day living by explaining and applying the mysteries of the faith to real life here and now—we can soon begin to advantageously place liturgical music and preaching into relationship with one another. We should note that knowing and sharing The Word within liturgy is intimately and inextricably linked to the daily lives of the faithful and our own knowing, loving, and sharing of The Word. Liturgical music, of course, can be a useful lens here too. First, though, let us detail the ways in which liturgical music and liturgical preaching are similar and dissimilar to one another.

Any detailed examination of any topic must begin with such unbiased description of small details before embarking on larger aspects of the project. Anne Lamott's *Bird by Bird* is the main primer for this approach, as is the need to begin any discussion at the bottom of Chris Argyris's Ladder of Inference, where one must first observe, select, and interpret data before coming to any conclusions and action steps. Another quick aside: the many divisions and misunderstandings in society and in the Church arise from neglecting the need for details and the necessity of starting conversations, especially tough ones, at the bottom of the Ladder of Inference. Without a set of common data points and a common vocabulary, anything that follows stands a large chance of being nearly pointless. But I digress.

Especially when considering psalms and hymns—that often have texts that utilize symbolism, imagery, and all of the other techniques found in good poetry—we should note that both preaching and liturgical music are meant to be communicative, dialogical, and relational. They both help to unpack scriptural lessons and theology in general and apply them to the Christian life, and when done well, they are both primarily spiritual rather than doctrinal.

I have, at times, had to sing a couple of hymns that I'd call doctrinal in nature; without naming titles or composers, they were flat-out terrible, as you might imagine.

Yet preaching is, at the same time, different than liturgical music. Music without words can express more of the ineffable divine mysteries by operating on the level of symbolism, with melodies, harmonies, rhythms, etc. each expressing more broadly what words, even poetic language, must do with more specificity. We've all experienced music that seems to be able to express emotions that words could only begin to describe or explain. If someone were to ask, "How are you today?" you might be able to answer them with the word "sad" or even something more particular like "melancholy," but playing them the first movement of Beethoven's "Moonlight Sonata" would likely give them an even better answer than any words would be able to accomplish. The piece's key, tempo, melodic pitches, harmonies in relation with one another, and so much more—all conscious choices by the composer, mind you—contribute to the music's expressivity. Imagine, though, if that musical answer was then given a text as well—that is, lyrics that it could amplify multiplicatively! (I know the musical *You're a Good Man, Charlie Brown* has already given the "Moonlight Sonata" lyrics, by the way, to great comedic and dramatic effect.)

Circling back, the emphasis that CSL places on "the mysteries of the faith" here, that this area of focus is specifically mentioned as an objective of the homily, will be an important inroad when it comes to putting liturgical music into conversation with preaching and any sharing of The Word. Much—though not all—of society today is rightly concerned with science. In the midst of a pandemic, global warming, other environmental issues, and more, we are urged to "follow the science," which in a way is to ask everyone to allow facts and findings to guide result-oriented actions. Science, however, at its core, is more about methodology and process than outcomes. Further, those outcomes often need human interpretations and judgments, at least when it comes to deciding what the data is telling us and how we might respond.

Science is, when reduced comically, about understanding whats and hows. Science tends to falter, in my experience, when faced with the question "Why?" When a curious and persistent two-year-old asks, "Why?" a few too many times in a row, at some point we are unable to come up with a good answer ("Because I said so" is typically not a good answer, I have learned). So too with the scientific method—though, to be fair, it never gives up trying.

Some today would tell us that science and faith are incompatible. On the contrary, faith and reason need one another, sometimes desperately. In my experience, faith—philosophy, really—handles the why well and frequently needs no recourse to the how to do so. Faith is content to let mysteries be mysteries. Further, faith even demands mystery. One cannot "believe" in a fact, after all; one must either accept it or deny it. One can believe, though, in things invisible and supernatural, in other people's motivations or proclivities, in God and the Trinity. In this day and age of the scientific method and humanity's search for answers almost exclusively through it, it is challenging, if not impossible, to allow faith to be true to itself and to instill the value of faith in others, most especially in the next generation of potential believers. Pope Francis, in *Desiderio Desideravi*, explains it this way:

> Guardini writes, "Here there is outlined the first task of the work of liturgical formation: man must become once again capable of symbols." This is a responsibility for all, for ordained ministers and the faithful alike. The task is not easy because modern man has become illiterate, no longer able to read symbols; it is almost as if their existence is not even suspected. . . . To have lost the capacity to grasp the symbolic value of the body and of every creature renders the symbolic language of the Liturgy almost inaccessible to the modern mentality. And yet there can be no question of renouncing such language. It cannot be renounced because it is how the Holy Trinity chose to reach us through the flesh of the Word. It is rather a question of recovering the capacity to use and understand the symbols of the Liturgy. (44)

Such is the current moment: Christian mystery is more important to embrace than ever while also more misunderstood and neglected than ever. Most of Christian mystery is embodied in paradox—death is life, weakness is strength, etc.—and the scientific method doesn't quite know what to do with paradox. While the scientific method certainly leaves itself open to further data points, new learnings, and updated results, the people doing science most often desire clear and certain results and are sometimes reluctant to enter into conversation and relationship with one another to achieve them. This can be for a variety of reasons: sometimes pride, sometimes capitalism, sometimes stubbornness. Within the house of God, faith *does* know what to do with paradox, how to express it and place it upon and within the hearts and minds of believers. Music and preaching, especially, communicate paradox so well because they are quite comfortable with it and have nothing to fear from embracing it or from the conversations and relationships both music and preaching need and create. Faith, particularly by music and preaching, creates communion not in spite of mystery and paradox but because of it, in gratitude for it, with no apology because of it.

This challenge—creating communion by means of mystery and paradox—is not a goal of Christian faith within liturgy alone. It is, really, a goal, *the* goal, of every moment of our lives. How can we believers strive to know and share The Word with one another outside of liturgy to the same ends as liturgical preaching has in its own context? How can we, moment to moment, endeavor to relationally uplift the faithful in their day-to-day living by explaining and applying the mysteries of the faith to real life here and now, especially by action, either alongside—or sometimes instead of—our words?

Paul wrote to the Ephesians, "So be imitators of God, as beloved children, and live in love, as Christ loved us and handed himself over for us as a sacrificial offering to God for a fragrant aroma" (5:1-2). The Greek word for this particular sacrificial love is *agape*. When John writes in his epistles that "God is love," again, the word in Greek is *agape*. Beyond these two scriptural examples, there are over two hundred uses of the word *agape* in the New Testament. One more practical, more tangible way to think of *agape* is that it is not a feeling. Rather, it is the impetus, the reason for living and loving in the sacrificial and covenantal way Christ loves us. We are called to *agape* love through Christ's example, which Paul wrote about above.

Agape necessitates loving beyond convenience. It means loving without counting the cost, without comparing, without conceit. We cannot *agape*-love God without *agape*-loving others. We must even *agape*-love our enemies. *Agape* is covenant, it is *chesed* (Hebrew for "mercy"). *Agape* is preaching the Gospel without words. This sort of love, which puts the well-being, even the salvation, of others ahead of our own, is the pinnacle of Christian love and the fullest form of sharing The Word in an effective way that bears witness to Christ and draws others to him.

Of course, many times it is necessary to use words to preach the Gospel, as limited and incomplete as they are in the service of transcendent mystery and divinity. What example might the faithful turn to as an example of how to preach The Word successfully when words are required?

There's a story about St. Dominic that's familiar to every Dominican—and we should quickly recall that the more formal, official name for these religious is the Order of Preachers. This story has important implications for us in this project too. Here is one telling of it that details particularly critical attributes:

> In the autumn of 1203 Dominic, a young canon of Osma cathedral, was travelling with his bishop Diego di Acebes on a diplomatic mission to Denmark on behalf of King Alfonso VIII of Castile. While passing through the south of France, he became aware of the social and religious confusion and turmoil in which the people of God found themselves on account of the Cathar heresy. . . . Providence led Dominic and his bishop Diego to stay in an inn whose owner adhered to the heresy. As a result, Dominic spent the whole night listening attentively to this man's words of anger and scorn

as he had a go at the Church, with its wealth and cozy relationship with those in power, and repeated the partial and categorically asserted truths touted by the heretics without stopping to consider or qualify them. Dominic listened attentively: he didn't just hear his host out, nor did he judge him, but rather showed his openness to him. This did not mean simply agreeing with him in order to be "nice" and thus confirming him in his way of thinking, but the exact opposite: he overturned the innkeeper's certainties one by one and calmed his anger. He pursued a real conversation, engaging the innkeeper on the level of reasoned arguments, illumined by the light of faith, and so helping him to distinguish the truth of the gospel message from its surrogates, which might be attractive but consistently fall short because of the simple fact that their god is created by man, and so does not exist. In this listening and the ensuing discussion, like Christ with the disciples on the way to Emmaus, . . . Dominic first breaks open the Word (cf Lk 24:27) until the innkeeper, like those disciples, recognizes the one true God revealed by Christ, passing from disappointment, error and a feeling of abandonment to the heartfelt joy of learning he has always been loved and never deceived (cf Lk 24:32). Like those disciples he realizes he thought he knew everything about Him but had never really met him or allowed the Son of God to take hold of him. After they had listened to that stranger on the way to Emmaus and accepted his word, those disciples discovered him to be the Christ, the necessary companion on their own earthly pilgrimage, and they decided to return to Jerusalem that very night, which was no longer night for them; likewise, the innkeeper would greet the dawn a different man. In fact, the breaking of the new day saw the birth of two new men: the innkeeper, converted to the true faith, and Dominic, who, moved by God, saw how necessary it was to help his neighbor to rediscover what is true, good and beautiful![2]

A most important component of this story, that St. Dominic helped the innkeeper to distinguish real truths from false ones, is mentioned almost in passing. There is a Dominican maxim, dating from early in the order's existence: "Never deny, seldom affirm, always distinguish." It's attributed to St. Thomas Aquinas and gives a framework for a path forward, especially when embarking on difficult discussions—which, of course, never happen in the world of liturgy or liturgical music (yes, that's sarcasm there).

By "never deny," what is meant here is that the listener should, by charity, assume the goodwill of the other and seek in what is being said even some partial truth, perhaps in one very specific detail or in an overarching sentiment—or possibly even in a "metamessage" behind the content. An example: if someone suggests needing more entertaining preaching to the point of absurd suggestions, like having the pastor learn magic tricks or dress up like a mime, the metamessage here might be that the preaching more broadly needs to be more engaging, more relevant, even if the proposed methodology is on shaky ground.

By "seldom affirm," the listener avoids traps by fully and only aligning on one side of any given discussion. It even disallows the avoidance technique of "agreeing to disagree" and forces those in conversation to further explore opportunities for better answers, more agreement.

The key clause is really the final one: "always distinguish." With this, the maxim allows all parties room to disagree while still seeking specific areas of agreement and truth. By mandating that the speaker chooses words carefully, discussion freely continues with mutual care and respect.

To put some flesh on these methodological bones, here are some helpful real-world phrases one might use. (Later in this book I'll offer some specific examples; for now, an exploration of the process will suffice.) Imagine someone presents you a rationale for a decision they made, with which you disagree. Perhaps included in their rationale is a generic reason that, borrowing from algebra, I'll call X. Your conversation partner knows what X is and what it means to them, but you realize that you don't know for sure what is in their heart and mind. Like algebra, you need to "solve for X." What do they mean by it? Is their definition of it the same

as yours? Is it too expansive or, perhaps, too limited? To help the
two of you sort that out, you might say things like

"If by X, you mean XYZ, then no; I see X meaning rather ABC";

"It would be helpful to distinguish here between X and Y"; and

"I believe X to be accurate but not necessarily a cause of Y."

Reflexive listening is also helpful here. "What I just heard you say
is . . ." is a useful phrase, as this technique—and any following
queries and distinctions—will ensure that both speaker and listener are in agreement as to what is being communicated.

If such discussions presume charity and a sincere desire to explore, communicate, and learn, then reason is also allowed into
the exchange of ideas, and both truth and community are allowed
to emerge from even the most divergent ideas and approaches. By
using this methodology to explore mystery and paradox, such a
pursuit truly becomes a way to both better know The Word and
more effectively share it: communication creating communion.

Similarly, the underlying nature of the liturgical homily as communicative and as a creator of communion among and within the
faithful ought to be another useful access point to that paradox
and mystery that is the heart of what faith is and, thus, is the heart
of the Christian faithful. Musical and poetic (lyrical) techniques
are most helpful at communicating mystery, expounding on unity,
and relationally bringing new insights into the human condition
and contexts. These techniques should also be able to inform and
influence both *agape* and the Dominican approach to conversations, which always distinguishes in the pursuit of truth and does
not shy away from mystery and paradox.

The question at hand, literally in your hands right now, is
whether liturgical preaching and our living and sharing The Word
today can learn and utilize any similar techniques and opportunities toward any similar outcomes. I believe they can, otherwise
this book wouldn't exist. We have arrived, then, at the crux of

this project: What can liturgical preaching and living The Word learn from exploring all the various elements and relationships of liturgical music and the liturgy itself, both for their betterment and for the greater holiness of the whole Church?

7

Exploring the Relationship between Music, Liturgy, and The Word

Acclamations and Responses

I began my life as a pastoral musician when I was ten years old, when it became known in my small Catholic church in my small hometown of Tyler, Minnesota, that I had been taking organ lessons for a few years and had reached a point where my skills might be sufficient to at least play for the Stations of the Cross that particular Lent. At these services, one only had to play the same simple and short six-measure hymn ("At the cross her station keeping . . ."—the STABAT MATER, for those who know hymn tunes) fifteen times over the course of some thirty minutes or so.

Later that fall I began to play at masses, at first under the mentorship of a couple of experienced adult accompanists. By the next spring, I was "flying solo" at masses, and a year later I was playing as many as thirty masses in a year. All that music we were making and praying with—all the texts, the rhythms, the harmonies, the melodies, the dynamics, the tempos, and the structures—began to embed itself within me and to form my faith and my understanding of the liturgy and the role of music as essential within it. I didn't, at the time, have the proper language to describe or name such things necessarily, but already my path down liturgical theology was beginning.

It wasn't until my college years that I began selecting music for the liturgy and began to arrange and compose some of my own music as well. It was at that time that I began to ponder the role of liturgical hymnody as, nearly, a second homily, another opportunity for nonprescribed texts to elaborate on and reinforce the other parts of the mass, most especially the scriptures. Inasmuch as music serves the practical needs of the liturgy, such as accompanying the various processions, there is indeed a particular responsibility for composers of liturgical music and texts, as well as for those who choose and implement the music for liturgy. Music ministers must understand this profound opportunity and approach it with reverence and awe—not to mention, more practically, a fair amount of formation, education, and sincerity.

This, too, is the goal here: to explore the various components of liturgical music—the texts, the rhythms, the harmonies, the melodies, the dynamics, the tempos, the forms and structures—for any potential similarities to the process of creating preaching texts and the effective delivery of them. That is, as already indicated, this is not a study of the use of music within preaching, though we will consider that briefly along the way. Rather, this is more about what preaching can learn from the various attributes of liturgical music and its execution and how preaching can utilize these new insights, likely without any music being involved.

Additionally, we will further investigate how sharing The Word happens outside the church doors and how the relationship of liturgical music, liturgy, and The Word itself can inform our day-to-day conversations and activities. To be a disciple is to be a student; to be a disciple of Christ is to be disciplined by him, to allow him to train us who call ourselves Christians to say and do things in a mindful, measured, and habitual way. We most fully come to know Christ by scripture, by the liturgy, and by how we live both of these each moment of every day. Music stands, then, not only as a lens through which to view all of this but as a binding mortar, as perhaps grace itself infused into all we say and do.

Acclamations

The first category of liturgical music, you'll recall, are acclamations, congregational outbursts of praise and assent. Chief among these are the Alleluia, which welcomes the words and deeds of Christ in our midst, and the Amen, our great assent to the whole of the eucharistic prayer, a prayer not only of the ordained minister but of the whole assembly. As outbursts, as expressions of praise and assent, these bits of music are brief, often repetitive, and are usually very energetic and loud. Composers are wise to give them melodies that congregations can easily grasp, in a high but still accessible range. Both the "Celtic Alleluia" (example 1 in the appendix), by Fintan O'Carroll and Christopher Walker, and the "Amen" from the *Mass of Creation* (example 2 in the appendix), by Marty Haugen, meet all these descriptors, which in part helps account for their widespread use and popularity.

Such outbursts of assent and praise, along with other similar congregational outbursts, are common in the Black Church in the United States. It is common to hear such assemblies respond with these specific (spoken) acclamations, in fact, to a preacher seeking their engagement, their permission, their agreement—which in actuality is the assembly engaging with Christ himself. Is there a role for acclamations, be they spoken or sung, in any preaching opportunities in other contexts and circumstances where such outbursts are less common?

Inasmuch as these acclamations within preaching would be an assembly's assent to the preacher's powerful words and to the activity of Christ in their midst, some assemblies will feel the need, consciously or not, to get permission from the preacher to engage with The Word in such a vocal and responsive way. Many congregations are quite used to sitting still and quietly during the preaching (or the sermon, the homily, whatever it may be called) and will not be used to doing something very different than that, especially unbidden.

A priest I used to work with, Fr. Raul Salas, OMI, would point out frequently in his homilies that if the congregation truly understood the truth of the resurrection and the truth of what was happening at the mass—and that those truths were one and the same—they would not be able to contain themselves; there would be raucous cries of joy and jubilant dancing right then and there. And, of course, he wasn't wrong about that. There are places on Earth where mass is celebrated by priest and assembly alike in just that way. That's not all places, though, and certainly not the experience (or the conditioning, one might say) that many of us may have in the United States.

If this is a technique one wishes to try, it may very well need to be introduced and catechized, and the assembly will likely need to be given permission by the preacher to offer acclamations without being asked to. This is a critical distinction between acclamations and responses: acclamations are offered without being asked. The Alleluia before the gospel arises liturgically from nothing. The presider doesn't ask for the assembly's assent at the conclusion of the doxology; rather, the assembly's "Amen" erupts in agreement with that trinitarian hymn of praise and the whole of the eucharistic action that preceded it.

Responses

Responses, on the other hand, are invited, usually as part of that scripted, stilted liturgical dialogue mentioned earlier (e.g., "The Lord be with you." "And with your spirit"). The dialogues during the Liturgy of the Word are even more abrupt, not even complete sentences: "The word of the Lord." "Thanks be to God." These phrases are instantly familiar to most any Catholic assembly, and the use of them or similar familiar back-and-forths embedded in preaching would be immediately effective in engaging a congregant's attention.

We likely all know that one scripture passage, the one that elicits a reflexive response every time it's read. For Catholics, it's on the Second Sunday in Ordinary Time, Cycle A, which is the beginning of Paul's first epistle to the Corinthians. It's his greeting to that community, the end of which reads, "Grace to you and peace from God our Father and the Lord Jesus Christ" (1 Cor 1:3). How many times—*how many times*—have we heard significant portions of our congregations hazily and half-heartedly respond to that phrase with some combination of "And with your spirit" and "And also with you"? That shows how powerful and useful responses are, rousing a complacent and unfocused assembly into at least some amount of attention and action.

It was popular in youth ministry circles for a while to use the call-and-response "God is good! All the time!" and "All the time! God is good!" to bring unfocused and talkative teens at a youth rally or a retreat, for instance, back to the speaker or activities at hand, and many from that generation, now older, still have a nearly unavoidable stimulus-response reaction to one of these calls.

Liturgical responses are meant to be sung, but they don't need to be and are often invariably spoken. Beyond the prescribed responses of the liturgy, some contemporary composers are finding ways to incorporate new responses into their compositions, allowing them to offer unique new ways to engage the assembly in dialogue, giving them a "lens" with which to view and interpret the whole of the content of the text of the piece.

One of these is "This Is How" by Chris de Silva (example 3 in the appendix). We can see and hear in this piece, in terms of its lyrics, how the refrain offers an initial frame for the rest of the song: Christ telling his disciples, and us today, in John 13:35 that the world will know that we are his disciples by our love for one another. We have perhaps seen similar content on social media. A common internet meme has the text "They'll know we are Christians by our . . ." at the top, followed by a list of characteristics, each crossed out: politics, infighting, name-calling, etc. At the bottom, not crossed out, is one single word: love.

Yet the word "love" here remains at least potentially ambiguous, amorphous: What is this Christian love exactly? What does it look like? What does it do? Is it *agape*, as discussed earlier? The verses of "This Is How" utilize a response from the assembly along with verses sung by the cantor or choir to, as a homily should, expound on the subject at hand. While the assembly repeats and responds, "This is how . . . ," the other text, sung by a single voice, tells us, "In the washing of the feet, in the breaking of the bread, in the feeding of the hungry. . . ." It is almost, in this instance, as if the assembly—recall that music ministers are part of the assembly too—is in dialogue with itself. This is a technique some preachers have tried—"Turn to your neighbor for a moment and answer the following question for each other"—with various amounts of success (and, yes, failure too).

With such a dialogical form, this sort of music is able to keep the assembly engaged by giving them and then returning them to a consistent viewpoint. Litanies, in some ways, are built with a similar structure, though they are typically much longer and involve often, as in the Litany of the Saints, a back-and-forth among music ministers and the rest of the assembly, all of whom are in conversation and dialogue with someone else (in this case, the saints of our faith). Litanies, because of their length and their form, evocative of mantras, work well in opening up two-way prayerful dialogue between heaven and earth.

"This Is How" does a fine job introducing its response (not quite a litany here) and committing to its repetition. Any similar use of this technique in preaching would need also to be well introduced, even taught first. The preacher must then commit with determination to the repetition of that response. One way to speed this process along is to give the homily a context familiar to an assembly, which invokes a frame of mind, if not an innate desire, to engage in such a responsive dialogue.

Here's a brief example: Many years ago, at an early afternoon Christmas Eve mass I was attending, the celebrant, following the gospel proclamation, invited all to be seated but also invited all the children between the ages of four and twelve to gather closer to him, in the area between the altar and the first pew. Meanwhile, a strong server procured a rocking chair hidden behind a sidewall and brought it out for the priest to sit in. I don't recall the name of the book, sadly, but the priest retrieved it from the table near his chair, sat down in the rocking chair, and began to read it to the children. It was a children's picture book about the birth of Christ, and each pair of pages ended with the same line of text—which, sadly, I don't recall either.

I do recall that while he taught that line to the children, he made a point of teaching it to the whole of the assembly as well. And while he read the simple story of the incarnation, it became clear that—of course—the homily was not just for that herd of children surrounding him but for us all, and that this congregational response he had taught us all was superb in keeping everyone engaged and attentive. This moment had become a sort of "Story Time with Grandpa Joe," if you will, and as such immediately gave the congregation a context to know what to expect and what to do along the way.

A last note about acclamations and responses: the latter can be used as a teaching tool to give an assembly both the permission and skills to use the former. That is, responses can be a stepping-stone toward assembly acclamations during preaching. Both acclamations and responses can have immediate positive effects: moving the assembly deeper into its full, conscious, and active role in the liturgy and fostering unity and communion between assembly and pastor by means of communication and dialogue. And, among the novel techniques to add to a preaching toolkit, these are likely the easiest to understand and implement successfully for both preacher and congregation. Let's look at another example of how this might be done, imagining the following text being preached within a community gathered for mass on Sunday morning.

Preaching example—use of responses:
"Here I Am, Lord"

Preaching on 1 Samuel 3:3b-10, 19—The Calling of Samuel
Catholic Lectionary, Cycle B, Second Sunday
in Ordinary Time [65]

What is the first thing you have a conscious memory of— not something your parents told you about later, or that you have video of, but something embedded in your own memory? Is it a favorite storybook or a television show? Perhaps a moment with a beloved pet or a unique experience from some out-of-town travels?

See if you can recall the first time you prayed in your own words—not with the familiar prayers of our faith, but in new and different words, words you made your own. Maybe that would be a moment here in church, or saying an improvised meal blessing at home, or bartering with God one day to get out of trouble, or praying as a last-ditch effort to get a pony for a certain Christmas long ago.

For me, it was when I was five years old.[1] My parents and my older sister and I were at Saturday evening mass at St. Dionysius Catholic Church in Tyler, Minnesota, one January. It was a few minutes before mass, and my father had the missalette open in his lap, set to the readings for mass. At age five, I was just learning to read, so what I saw on these pages didn't mean very much to me, but there was an image on one of the pages that captured my imagination like nothing else in church ever had up to that point.

It was a sort of stick figure drawing, but one could tell that the figure, a human, had their head slightly raised and was reaching both hands up to the heavens. As I pondered this image, I couldn't help but feel like it was trying to tell me something, like there was something I needed to take away from that moment. Then I realized there were a few words underneath the image: the caption.

Now, this is the part of my story where you all need to play the role of my dad. And you've already rehearsed your line! It was our responsorial psalm today, beautifully led by our choir. If, somehow, you've already forgotten it, you'll find it at the bottom of page seventy-four in our hymnals. And don't worry—you'll know exactly when it's time for the line; I'll let you know.

Back to our story: I leaned over to whisper in Dad's ear and asked, "What does that say, right there?" pointing with my finger. And he whispered back *[gesture toward assembly]*,

Assembly: "Here I am, Lord; I come to do your will."

That was pretty well done, but it was rather loud actually. Remember, this was just a few minutes before mass, a very quiet moment! So, I leaned over to whisper in Dad's ear, "What does that say, right there?" And he *whispered* back *[gesture toward assembly]*,

Assembly: "Here I am, Lord; I come to do your will."

Much better. Yes, here I am, Lord; I come to do your will. Now, I don't know how you imagine the inner workings of your brain; I like to imagine mine as a hamster running on one of those exercise wheels—the harder I'm thinking the faster he has to run. And at this point, my hamster is nearly ready to collapse from so much exertion! What does all this mean? What is this image? What are these words trying to tell me?

And, suddenly, the lightbulb goes off: I'm being taught a new way to pray. I'm sure I already knew to some extent the common prayers of our faith, from the rosary and such, but this seemed to me to be something new, something that I could pray, could make my own—and then expect an answer back from God! I would just strike that pose from the image and say *[gesture toward assembly]*,

Assembly: "Here I am, Lord; I come to do your will."

And then God would answer me: "Well, today, Steven, I need you to clean up your room, help with the dishes after dinner, and try not to annoy your older sister so much." Now, I wasn't actually sure if God would answer me with a big booming voice or exactly how, but five-year-old me was pretty darn sure *something* would happen.

So on Monday I decided to try it out. My father, a schoolteacher, was at work, and my sister was at school too, so I told my mom I was going outside to play. I mentioned in passing earlier that this was in Minnesota, and hopefully you've figured out that this scene took place this very same weekend, though many years ago. I don't know if any of you have experienced a Minnesota January, but it's a bit odd to go outside and play in the cold winter if you don't have to, if you're not forced out by your parents so they can get a little peace and quiet.

But outside I went. And, right at the bottom of the steps, I stretched my hands up to the sky, as I remembered from the image, and recalling the words my father had whispered in my ear *[gesture toward assembly]*—

Assembly: "Here I am, Lord; I come to do your will."

—with all my heart, I prayed, "Here I am, Lord; I come to do your will!"

And do you know what happened? Nothing! Nothing that I could discern, anyway. There were the gray winter clouds wafting along and the barren branches of the maple tree lightly swaying in the breeze. But there was no big, booming voice, no answer to my prayer as I had expected, as far as I could tell.

So I began to wonder what was going wrong. I was pretty sure I remembered the image correctly and knew I had the words right, so maybe I was just in the wrong spot. I ran over to one corner of the backyard and tried again *[gesture toward assembly]*:

Assembly: "Here I am, Lord; I come to do your will."

And then to another corner *[gesture toward assembly]*:

Assembly: "Here I am, Lord; I come to do your will."

And then to three or four other places *[gesture toward assembly three times in rapid succession]:*

Assembly: "Here I am, Lord; I come to do your will. Here I am, Lord; I come to do your will. Here I am, Lord; I come to do your will."

And each time I got nothing in response. Nothing at all.

Now, when you're five years old, you don't spend too much time dwelling on moments like this. I don't recall exactly, but I wasn't outside very long, likely only a few minutes. I went back inside and probably found a Christmas toy from a few weeks earlier to play with. But there hasn't been more than a month or two of my life that's gone by where I haven't thought back to those Minnesotan days and their significance in my life.

On my own journey of faith, these memories have meant different things to me at different times. Initially, this episode meant something like, "Perhaps God doesn't really notice people like little ol' me." Then, into my teenage years, it meant something more like "maybe there isn't a God up there to notice me at all."

Today, as I recall those moments of my life, I think I was looking for the answer to my prayer in the wrong spot. Very few of us, nearly none of us, really, get to experience God as a big, booming voice or, like Moses did, in the burning bush. So what can we do to be attentive to God, to God's words and activities in our world today?

We know from the first chapters of Genesis that we are all made in the image and likeness of God, and Paul's epistles tell us that we are created as "temples of the Holy Spirit," to be a fleshly dwelling for the divine presence. Take a moment and glance at the person who may be sitting to your left, to your right, in front of you, and behind you. Each of these people were created in the image and likeness of God, created to be a temple of the Holy Spirit; each of these people might be someone whom God uses to say something today, to do something today to become more present to any one of us. It might be as simple as a friendly greeting or holding the door for someone. And while you were looking at three or four people just now, three or four people were looking at you! You might be the answer to someone's prayer today without even realizing it.

It took Samuel several iterations of being woken up by who he thought was Eli to sort out what was really happening, and so it may be for us when we set our focus on doing the Lord's will, on letting God direct our speech and our actions. Don't be discouraged if living by God's truth and responding to God's call brings obstacles, difficulties, and frustrations into our lives. Rather, let Samuel teach us the same prayer my father inadvertently taught me *[gesture toward assembly]*:

Assembly: "Here I am, Lord; I come to do your will."

And let each of us be willing, as I was and still am, to take another step toward God, with God, on our own journeys of faith. This is all that God desires: for each of us to stay on the path to holiness; to be willing to align our wills more closely to the divine will; to always be able—with courage, trust, and determination—to respond lovingly and freely to God's call to each of us *[gesture toward assembly]*:

Assembly: "Here I am, Lord; I come to do your will."

We can also apply our reflections on acclamations and responses to what they might offer us who desire to live and share The Word outside of the liturgical experience. Let us first return to what *agape* love can bring into relationship with acclamations and responses. We will recall that *agape* is sacrificial and unconditional, and because of these attributes it is the love most needed by those in any particular crisis and, especially, by those on the margins. Those who are in positions of power or normative social structures most especially do well to listen, understand, and learn. While not a sacrifice per se, giving up one's voice to make room for voices underheard and cast aside is Christlike love, without a doubt. When in a position to do so, our task is to seek out such under-represented voices and offer acclamations of assent to them: "Yes! Preach it! More!" We turn as well to others like ourselves to say, "Listen to this! Amazing!" and the like.

In more intimate circumstances, listening is a largely undeveloped skill—listening, that is, to truly understand and learn rather than listening to form a rebuttal. We can recall that the Greek word *homilia* points toward relational union through an exchange of ideas rather than speech that is only transactional or heard only to craft a reply. One of the first techniques many marriage counselors teach to couples trying to repair broken relationships is reflexive listening, already mentioned earlier, which we shall see is very much like a liturgical musical response. While many of those responses are stilted and scripted because it's the nature of our liturgy to be precisely ordered and familiar, the responses that reflexive listening desires depend on close listening to one another. Imagine a scenario where a college student asks to speak to a professor following class one day:

> Student: "What Alicia said in class earlier offended me. She didn't even try to see it from my perspective or anybody else's. Isn't this whole class about evaluating different perspectives? She failed."
>
> Professor: "I hear you saying that what Alicia said has hit a nerve with you. It doesn't speak to your personal experience or to what you're trying to get out of the class. You're not sure what to do next."

Here, the professor has listened closely to the student and is attempting to reassure her that they are hearing and understanding the concern. This style of listening and responding serves many valuable purposes. First, it makes the speaker (in this case, the student) know and feel that they are being heard. It also opens the door to the Dominican method of pursuing truth: seldom affirming, never denying, and always distinguishing. It allows the student to clarify anything the professor has misunderstood. This approach also moves both parties in the conversation closer to the bottom of the Ladder of Influence that we discussed earlier, which is almost always beneficial.

> Student: "Yes, thank you. I do have an idea what to do though. I'd like to speak with her one on one and see if she is receptive to hearing my concerns."

> Professor: "You desire direct communication with Alicia and want to resolve the difficulties and repair the relationship. Do you think my presence at that conversation would be helpful?"

The professor here, by close listening, is able to create helpful responses utilizing reflexive listening. Such responses, alongside *agape* love and the Dominican way of seeking truth, help create community and communion and uplift the community by sharing The Word without even a direct appeal to scripture. Instead, the Word is shared by living the Eternal Logos in speech and deed.

8

Exploring the Relationship between Music, Liturgy, and The Word

Psalms and Antiphons

Attentive readers will have already noticed that the preaching example in chapter seven relies heavily on a psalm—Psalm 40. Because the story shared within the preaching referenced the preacher's faith journey, including psalmody within the sample homily was a perfect fit. So many of the psalms are within themselves a journey of faith, frequently a journey from defeat, dejection, failure, and lament to (by turning again to the Lord) hope, joy, promise, and new life. Psalm 130, which begins, "Out of the depths I call to you," is a classic example of this kind of journey of faith, for both the author and reader—or singer—of that text.

However, the responsorial psalms at mass, and the way that psalms are used as or with the proper antiphons for each liturgy, frequently only give us a small fraction of the complete text of a given psalm. Consider, for instance, that while Psalm 117 has but 25 words in our current liturgical translation, some psalms are, on the other hand, very long: Psalm 119 has over 2,000 words across 176 verses!

The way that a particular antiphon—more commonly called a refrain—can affect our hearing and understanding of a psalm when linked to a larger segment of it is immense and perhaps even an outsized betrayal of the psalm in its fullness. Consider

Palm Sunday's Psalm 22; its verses take the singer on a journey from lament to hope and praise, while the refrain text that follows every verse, "My God, why have you abandoned me?" is firmly entrenched in sorrowful neglect. When music is also attached to these psalm texts, attributes like key, tempo, and meter, along with the melodic arcs and harmonic shifts present, can greatly impact how the psalm is performed and received, how the significance of it is amplified, how it is "prayed twice."

Similarly, consider Psalm 34, which is represented in the appendix (examples 4 and 5). First, we look at the text of each refrain: "Taste and see the goodness of the Lord" and "The Lord hears the cry of the poor." Similar to how the refrain of our previous musical example ("This Is How") worked, these words create a frame for the rest of the song. They also, on their own, greatly shift the reception and perception of the words of the verses. Our two examples even share the same words in verse one, differing only mildly in their adaptations. The differing refrains place us, as singer or listener, into very different spiritual spaces, which in turn completely change the spiritual interpretation of these same words in verse one.

Next, we can layer the music on top of the texts of both refrains and both first verses. We will immediately notice that several details in the refrain of "Taste and See" (example 4) by James Moore, Jr., stand in contrast to the other setting. Here, we have a major, perhaps even cheery, key and a pulse akin to a walking tempo or speed (andante, for those "in the biz"). We have harmonies that are almost all major and a melodic arc that uses the lengthy expanse of the refrain to rise and eventually fall back to where it began. In "The Cry of the Poor" (example 5) by John Foley, SJ, almost everything is different—still beautiful in its own way, I would note, but very different. The key is minor and dolorous, the tempo has a slower "cut time" pulse, which feels rather like a resting, slow heartbeat. The harmonies are minor, too, even modal at times, which gives the refrain an intentionally antiquated feeling, perhaps. The melodic arc is also purposefully abbreviated compared to example 4, with less melodic "distance" to travel, in a more confined range, in a way almost limiting the expressive possibilities of the tune, which in turn makes the piece seek communicative meaning elsewhere, in harmony, dynamics, and other expressive tools. Both pieces notably give longer notes to more important words and shorter notes to less important ones, a common practice to emphasize and de-emphasize the text when desired.

Even more contrast musically is found in verse one of each piece even though the text is largely the same. Even looking only at the first phrase, "I will bless the Lord at all times," melodically, in "Taste and See" the phrase starts on a low pitch so it can rise in praise and exuberance, while in "The Cry of the Poor," we again find a limited vocal range. It returns, almost begrudgingly, to where it began—or perhaps that melodic arc is, again, purposefully indicative of an inability on behalf of our "narrator," as it were, to be any more joyful about their praise of God at this particular moment.

As the verses continue, we can note that, musically, each piece gives us some unexpected harmonic interest in different ways. Most interestingly, the verse of "Taste and See" ends on what is called a half cadence, giving it a feeling of being unfinished, which in this case propels the singer back into the refrain. The verse of "The Cry of the Poor" has a wonderfully expressive and unexpected chord progression about two-thirds of the way through, but also ends harmonically where it began (on the tonic), so the end of any verse could actually be the end of the piece if it wanted to be, without the need for another refrain.

Details such as these are embedded into the pieces at the compositional stage, though some aspects of any performance can, and sometimes should, be altered by the performers. The tempo and pacing of the piece (and any amounts of adjustment to that pacing as the piece is performed) along with variation in dynamics are the most obvious places an accompanist or singer can affect a piece as it is being performed. Especially when singing a psalm, attentiveness to all these details is crucial to help impart the profound meaning of the text the music is carrying—particularly if the text is not a monolithic hymn of praise but rather an amalgamation of the many possible elements of a faith journey: lament, despair, return, trust, hope, and new life.

Many of these same musical attributes can, with attention, care, and practice, become part of our preaching as well, at both the compositional stage as well as when practicing its delivery and actually doing so as part of prayer. The human voice is so expressive to begin with; music is, in some respects, just a way of codifying and scripting that expressiveness. If we learn to become aware of how we can vary the timbre of our voice, the pacing and volume of our delivery, and even the pitch—the rising and falling—of our voice, these components can then begin to amplify the "naked" words of our texts in ways we perhaps thought only music could.

Consider the following exercise: I invite you to ask me to a friendly dinner tonight, and you do so. I respond, somewhat quickly, my voice in a higher range, and with indicated emphasis: "*That's* a great idea!" Then, however, I immediately ask you to repeat the invitation, and you do, but this time I respond a bit more slowly, at a more moderate pitch and pace, with different emphasis: "That's a *great* idea." I might even cross my arms and roll my eyes the second time to ensure you don't miss the sarcasm. Here, just like the first verses of our two examples of Psalm 34, we have the same words, but by varying the more or less musical qualities of the manner of responding, we completely change the meaning and significance of them.

We should quickly note, especially for the musically inclined, that changing such attributes of a piece of music or preaching presentation is not always a one-for-one exchange. That is, minor and slow doesn't always mean "sad," and fast and major doesn't always mean "happy." Indeed, a slow piece of music could also indicate or impart peacefulness or rest, and a fast piece of music might indicate or impart anger or panic. Plenty of joyful dance music is written in minor keys—think, for instance, of festive Jewish music.

Consider that Lent, our season of repentance in preparation for Easter, leads many music ministers to create or choose music that is slow or in a minor, morose key. Yet our liturgy itself, in its Preface I of Lent, says,

> [B]y your gracious gift each year
> your faithful await the sacred paschal feasts
> with the *joy* of minds made pure . . .
> (emphasis added)

If we follow the liturgical axiom *lex orandi, lex credendi*—"the law of prayer is the law of belief"—then Lent can or ought to be a season of joyful hope and expectation. *Lex orandi, lex credendi* should, then, either alter the renditions of music picked or lead composers to create and ministers to pick music that is truer to the complex nature of the sacred time.

Indeed, *lex orandi, lex credendi* should be a guiding principle for anyone charged with picking liturgical texts (sung or otherwise) or creating preaching. Consider the heavy weight of responsibility here: what we believe is what we pray; what we pray is what we believe. One can be reasonably sure (some would say certain) that the texts of the Missal itself give one sure footing. When creating or choosing hymn texts, for instance, one must be completely sure that these words, which will be prayed together, are accurate not only to the deposit of faith but to the lived experiences of the congregation that will enunciate them.

We'll talk more about the challenges of aligning hymn texts to our faith's doctrines and dogmas later on; just for a moment here, consider the challenge of finding a hymn text or creating a bit of preaching that meets every single congregant where they are at individually and speaks to and uplifts them in a meaningful and sincere way. One could argue that successfully meeting that challenge is impossible. It's certainly difficult, but I hope this text, as it continues to its end, shows that it's not impossible. Many of our psalms, for instance, reveal that their author is on a spiritual pilgrimage, as are we all. With these, it becomes a matter of knowing ourselves well and recognizing ourselves somewhere on that same journey that we are reading and praying with, hearing, or singing. Acknowledging to your assembly that you, as a preacher, recognize that your own journey and each of theirs is qualitatively different is so important. Allowing the assembly to find some element of their journey in yours—that's the key, along with acknowledging that it makes no difference to you where each person might be on their journey, just that they are "on the road," so to speak, and willing to take one more step toward God, with God. This is truly the heart of *lex orandi, lex credendi* when we get right down to it and is what allows our individual journeys to become one common journey of faith, as Church. That pilgrimage is what our entire earthly life is about, is for. Because of this, some even add *lex vivendi*—"the law of living"—to the law of prayer and belief.

Pope Francis made these same connections, in praise of (and perhaps even in defense of) the liturgy of Vatican II:

> If the liturgy is "the summit toward which the activity of the Church is directed, and at the same time the font from which all her power flows" (*Sacrosanctum Concilium*, n. 10), well then, we can understand what is at stake in the liturgical question. It would be trivial to read the tensions, unfortunately present around the celebration, as a simple divergence between different tastes concerning a particular ritual form. The problematic [sic] is primarily ecclesiological. I do not see how it is possible to say that one recognizes the validity of the Council—though it amazes me that a Catholic might presume not to do so—and at the same time not accept the liturgical reform born out of *Sacrosanctum Concilium*, a document that expresses the reality of the Liturgy intimately joined to the vision of Church so admirably described in *Lumen gentium*. For this reason, as I already expressed in my letter to all the bishops, I have felt it my duty to affirm that "The liturgical books promulgated by Saint Paul VI and Saint John Paul II, in conformity with the decrees of Vatican Council II, are the unique expression of the *lex orandi* of the Roman Rite." (*Desiderio Desideravi* 31)

To reiterate: what an awesome responsibility those of us who prepare liturgy and liturgical music have! Each aspect of our liturgies is interwoven with what it is we believe and how it is we live. Indeed, the fullness of all three liturgical components (prayer, belief, and life) is always inextricably linked and present in each moment of our individual and communal journeys of faith.

Psalm texts, those that present us with a spiritual journey, also show us that preaching should be careful not to exist in a "spiritual vacuum," so to speak. That is, the preaching on, for instance, the texts of Holy Week can't exist as if we don't know the end of the story—at least, the end of the story so far. It is, frankly, irresponsible to preach on suffering and death without also bringing in facets of resurrection and new life. It's also negligent to preach on renewal and vivification without noting some amount of sacrifice, suffering, and death. "Cheap grace," German theologian Dietrich Bonhoeffer would call it; more colloquially, Archbishop Fulton J. Sheen would explain, "Unless there is a Good Friday in your life, there can be no Easter Sunday." Faith is a journey, and our music and preaching should reflect, as best it can, the totality of that journey.

So, much like with music, our preaching should have, at the compositional phase, elements of key, tempo, meter, and other attributes at least considered if not written explicitly into it, and then it should be faithfully executed when that preaching is offered at prayer. Moreover, these elements must encompass a wide variety of highs and lows, responsive to the text and its treatment by the preacher. Doing so will not only multiplicatively extend the meaning and significance of the words themselves; it will also engage and retain the attention of an assembly whose attention spans grow ever shorter and whose experiences with multimedia grow ever wider. Here is another brief example of what enacting these principles might look like in practice.

Preaching example—use of musical elements as often found
in psalmody:
"Ask the Wrong Question, Get the Wrong Answer"

Preaching on Luke 13:22-30—Strive to Enter through
the Narrow Gate
Catholic Lectionary, Cycle C, Twenty-First Sunday in
Ordinary Time [123]

[For the purposes of this preaching example, we'll focus on
variations of dynamics (louder, softer) and pacing (quicker,
slower). In the text, a louder dynamic will be represented by
bold text, while a softer dynamic will be represented in *ital-
ics*. A faster-paced section of text will be in this narrow font,
while a slower section will be in this wide font. Some
bits of text **will** be *both*! Plain text like this will represent
average volume and pacing.]

A wise person once told me, "If you ask the wrong question, you get the wrong answer." Here's an example. Suppose
you walk down to the river one day only to see a baby floating his
way down the stream in a wicker basket. You can just barely reach
out to snag the basket and save the child before another basket
heads your way from upstream. You quickly find a place to set the
first baby down safely and race back to save the next—and when
you do, you see another. Followed by another. And another. You look
around for help, but you find yourself all alone.

As you frantically work to save all the children in the river, you think to
yourself, **"Surely there's got to be someone around to help me!
There must be a better way to save all these babies!"** These aren't
bad considerations, of course. But the pressing nature of the situa-
tion prevents you from considering an even more important question: "How are all these babies ending up in the river in
the first place?"

In today's gospel, someone asks a "wrong question" of Jesus:
"Lord, will only a few people be saved?" With a mastery seen only

among some of the "best" political candidates of our day, Jesus doesn't really answer that question. Instead, he answers the one he really wants to talk about.

It's not about how many will be saved but about the sorts of people, or rather *the sorts of faithfulness among God's people*, that are important when it comes to salvation. Salvation is a gift given to all; it's nothing we can earn. We do, however, have to accept that gift and, beyond that, make sure that all people know the gift of salvation that is there to be received. **"Go out to all the world and tell the Good News,"** the psalm instructs us. Our salvation as an individual is for naught if we don't strive for the salvation of the whole community.

Jesus gives, through parables, some instructions on living a Christian life; the epistles remind us to allow ourselves to be formed and shaped by those around us (and, in fact, by God) into a Christian people. So too we are to help others live a Christian life—by evangelization, catechesis, discipline, and *most of all, love.*

It's the wrong question but, in this case, the right answer: **Will only a few people be saved?** Our scriptures this weekend seem to make it clear that in some measure, the answer to that question is up to each of us. *Are you and I ready, right now, to answer that question, by our words and deeds?*

If we ponder these same musical attributes of dynamics and pacing and their potential intentional uses in sharing The Word in day-to-day living, the book of Ecclesiastes may come to mind:

There is an appointed time for everything,
    and a time for every affair under the heavens.
A time to give birth, and a time to die;
    a time to plant, and a time to uproot the plant.
A time to kill, and a time to heal;
    a time to tear down, and a time to build.

A time to weep, and a time to laugh;
   a time to mourn, and a time to dance.
A time to scatter stones, and a time to gather them;
   a time to embrace, and a time to be far from embraces.
A time to seek, and a time to lose;
   a time to keep, and a time to cast away.
A time to rend, and a time to sew;
   a time to be silent, and a time to speak.
A time to love, and a time to hate;
   a time of war, and a time of peace.
(Eccl 3:1-8)

Already noting that there is a time to be silent and a time to speak, we might append that there are times to speak loudly and speak quietly, that there are times to speak with words and without words, and that there are times to speak and act quickly and speak and act slowly. The contrast to that is the missing middle ground: when are the times to speak (and act) at a moderate volume, at a moderate pace? I'm fond of the axiom offered by Oscar Wilde: "Everything in moderation—including moderation."

This is in fact true of Christian virtues as well. A virtue, in reality, is a moderate position between a pair of vices: the absence of a particular virtue and the excess of that same one. Consider humility as a virtue. The absence of it is pride, one of the deadly sins. Yet it is possible (if rather difficult) to be too humble. James 4:10 and 1 Peter 5:6 plainly tell us to humble ourselves, but not the sort of humility that presupposes that we are too far gone to be saved, for instance, or unworthy to be a leader or an example of holiness to others. The absence of chastity is lust, another deadly sin, but too much chastity denies the gift of loving human sexuality and the unitive and creative aspects of that type of love.

The Christian virtue of temperance "is the moral virtue that moderates the attraction of pleasures and provides balance in the use of created goods. It ensures the will's mastery over instincts and keeps desires within the limits of what is honorable. The temperate person directs the sensitive appetites toward what is good and maintains a healthy discretion" (*Catechism of the Catholic Church* 1809).

In consideration of Mary and Martha in the familiar gospel of their offering different types of hospitality to Jesus, we must remind ourselves that our calling is not, broadly, to always be either "a Mary" or "a Martha," even though Jesus says that Mary has chosen the better part. Rather, we should be mindful that hospitality takes many forms and relies on certain gifts that each of us has in differing ways, at different times, and much of the time a more moderate and balanced approach is required and healthy.

Temperance, as described above, is the virtue that helps provide that sense of balance—not just in pursuit and use of "goods" but in all our daily living. In fact, the *Catechism* goes on to quote St. Augustine in that regard: "To live well is nothing other than to love God with all one's heart, with all one's soul and with all one's efforts; from this it comes about that love is kept whole and uncorrupted (through temperance). No misfortune can disturb it (and this is fortitude). It obeys only [God] (and this is justice), and is careful in discerning things, so as not to be surprised by deceit or trickery (and this is prudence)" (1809).

This particular cardinal virtue can impact how we approach all we say and do and so influences how we might carry out any particular liturgical ministry, for instance, but also any interaction in any time and any place. Especially if our role in our workplace is one of making critical decisions, it is almost always wise to ensure not only that a decision is reached with all the information and potential consequences in front of us but also that our disposition in that moment of deciding is one of balance and moderation.

One way of living temperance, balance, and moderation is (more secularly) embodied in the Virtue Continuum, as created by Jim Lanctot in 2007. Temperance is one of seven virtues on the continuum, which lists for each virtue extremes of "deficiency" and "excess," similar to the way some Christian virtues were described just above. A deficiency of temperance leads to licentiousness; an excess of temperance leads to strictness. Neither is healthy or good, yet again illustrating the saying "Everything in moderation, including moderation." I encourage you to explore the rest of the Virtue Continuum as you are able.

For the moment, ponder how temperance, balance, and moderation can better serve your sharing of The Word by framing your approach to each interaction and decision a day might set before you. One of the goals of any liturgical ministry, for instance, is to better create, form, and hold together the Christian community. If liturgy and life are inseparable, then our living, too, must share these same goals. There are, to return to the musical metaphor, times to speak loudly and times to speak quietly, times to communicate with words and times to communicate without words, and times to speak and act quickly and times to speak and act slowly. More often, though, our goal of building the reign of God on Earth will be best served not by extremism or zealotry but by love, mercy, and communion.

9

Exploring the Relationship between Music, Liturgy, and The Word

Songs and Hymns

The songs and hymns that are frequent pillars of most parishes' liturgies are tremendously variant in most every possible way. In terms of text, they might be scriptural, theological, devotional, or some combination of these. They might have many or few words, might rhyme or not, might have consistent meter or not, might utilize a refrain or not, might be monolingual or multilingual, and on and on and on.

The music to which these texts is set are just as varied. A composition might envision accompaniment by organ, piano, guitar, strings, or any other instrumentation suitable for liturgy—or no accompaniment at all! It might score out unison singing or four-part harmony; it might take the style of a march, a love ballad, any number of dance rhythms, a folk melody, or a beautiful art song. It might sound distinctly of a particular culture or region, or it might sound as if sung by cherubs joyfully, eternally worshiping around God's throne.

I will reiterate something already mentioned many pages ago because it is important: for the purpose of this project, these attributes are not especially important. What is important is that high-quality liturgical music arises from all times throughout Christian history and from as many places and cultures as there ever have been or ever will be. The craft of composing good music and, in particular, good liturgical music, ultimately, is the same no matter the time, place, or style.

One of the foundational elements of crafting an effective piece of music is maintaining a balance between meeting and denying the musical expectations of the performer and the listener. A piece of music that only meets musical expectations quickly becomes dull and boring. A piece of music that only offers musical surprises of pitch, harmony, or rhythm is challenging for a singer, especially one untrained in the pews, to learn and appreciate and is difficult to listen to. Obviously, when a piece of music is practiced enough, the surprise of a certain pitch or chord may fade but is, in reality, still there, especially if the piece, like a hymn for mass, is only used once every few months. Either approach will, in the end, detract from the text and its delivery (of paramount importance, especially at liturgy). A balance between expectation and surprise is key.

Many hymn tunes, especially but not exclusively older ones, utilize a structural format that is borrowed from sonata or symphonic forms. This format strikes a good balance, structurally, between meeting and denying musical expectations. My friend Christian Cosas, himself a fine composer of contemporary liturgical music, describes it this way: First, there is a musical statement—in the case of hymnody, often the first four-bar phrase. Second, there is some development of that statement, perhaps a repetition of it with minor melodic or harmonic changes. Third, there is something different injected into the piece that contrasts with anything we have heard so far. Fourth, and lastly, there is something that brings the piece "home" to a satisfying conclusion; this might be as straightforward as repeating one of the first two phrases of music.

The familiar "Ode to Joy" (HYMN TO JOY) tune by Beethoven (example 6, "Alleluia! Alleluia," in the appendix) is a good example of both of these elements of composition: the balance of meeting and denying expectations and the fourfold form just described. The first phrase of the tune has a predictable stepwise motion over two chords of music. The second phrase begins similarly but introduces a new chord underneath as well as new pitches to end the phrase. The third phrase of music is wholly different, introducing some leaps into the tune as well as some harmonies outside the key of the piece as a whole. The fourth phrase (in our hymnals, anyway) is an exact repeat of the second phrase, to bring the composition "home." I say "in our hymnals, anyway," because in Beethoven's original, the conclusion of the famous Ninth Symphony, that fourth phrase begins a very surprising one beat earlier than expected—a moment deemed too surprising for the typical pew-dweller, most arrangers and hymnal editors seem to have agreed.

It should be with our liturgical preaching, then, that we take care to make sure the content of it—as well as the delivery of it—usually meets expectations (but doesn't always) and has some sort of structure to it, be it borrowed from classical music or elsewhere. This could be as simple as having a common saying used from homily to homily, but one time, for particular cause and emphasis, changing the last word or two. Or it could be, in terms of structure, making sure to vary the style and tone of both the content and delivery around halfway through to effectively give an assembly member's ears something new to tune in to. Those with more musical knowledge will know there are countless other musical forms that might inform the structure of a homily too: What would a preaching sound and feel like if structured in rondo form, or as theme and variations? The possibilities are nearly endless.

There can also be a certain delight to our sharing of The Word in our daily interactions if we take care that the way we present ourselves and communicate with others is, on one hand, always the same and, on the other hand, never the same. Recall Christ's healing ministry: he is always careful to meet each person, and their faith, wherever they are, which means each interaction is a bit different, and each person's experience of the divine is a bit different too. To one, Jesus says, "Do you believe that I can do this?" (Matt 9:28), and to others in whom he already saw faith, he proceeded directly to words of healing. Yet he leads all to the same place: healing and restoration—of body, spirit, and community.

Sometimes Christ, when approached for a miracle, appears to be indifferent: "[H]ow does your concern affect me?" he asks his own mother at Cana (John 2:4). In one telling of the feeding of the multitudes, he turns the request back onto his disciples: "There is no need for them to go away; give them some food yourselves" (Matt 14:16). Ultimately, as Christ is *agape*, each miracle is eventually performed, not only as a tangible manifestation of his divinity, but out of his sacrificial and covenantal concern for the faithful. So too our *agape* for one another need not always look and feel the same—but it must have at its core loving one another as Christ loved and continues to love us.

If we pause here for a moment to consider the type of music that is to be afforded pride of place in our worship, there is also something that preaching can learn from Gregorian chant. These pieces of music follow very closely the rhythms of speech, or at least they should. Too often we experience chant as a bit slow, lugubrious, with equal emphasis and volume on each note and syllable. Put plainly, this is wrong. Chant has much more vitality and is truer to itself when it is allowed to pulse both rhythmically and dynamically with the natural speech rhythms of the text that it is setting.

The preaching that we offer must also be true to our own selves, the preachers, with obvious integrity and a consistency with who we are outside of the homily and, indeed, outside of the liturgy. There seem to be many in seminaries who are being taught, not incorrectly, that their presiding and preaching must not be used to call undue attention to themselves and should only point to Christ. After all, while the liturgy is rightly called *performative*, it is at the same time not *performance*. In agreement with this premise, let me simultaneously observe that the way to reach that laudable end is not to make one's preaching and presiding as bland and unexciting as possible. Rather, this approach calls even more attention to itself than do some presiders who might be accused of being too gregarious and attention seeking during their liturgical ministries. (We should also recall here the earlier mentioned "poorly concealed mania to be the centre of attention" that Pope Francis describes in *Desiderio Desideravi* 54.) In the words of Polonius, given him by William Shakespeare, "This above all: to thine own self be true." Enough said.

Turning now to language, we remind ourselves that preaching exists to expound upon the mysteries of the faith. As such, songs and hymns can remind us that poetic language is most often valuable when breaking open such mysteries. Poetry is capable of this because good poetry itself already resides in the sphere of mystery, symbolism, metaphor, analogy, synecdoche, and the like. There is a good reason Jesus taught principally in parables, which frequently use more or less similar techniques as poetry. A parable draws you in, allows you to hold it beside your own life experiences and that of the whole community and seek divine wisdom and understanding there. Poetry, written well, does this too.

More on this a bit later, though. For now, an example to suffice (example 7, "I Give My Spirit," in the appendix). My friend Shannon Cerneka and I wanted to write a setting of Psalm 31 that could be used, in some manner, on Good Friday. My first suggestion for a refrain text for this piece is not what you see here. Instead, I had used the word "dead" where you see the word "lifeless." "Dead" might be a more accurate word, but it is rather abrupt and not poetic, and our attempts to set it to music quickly failed. Shannon suggested using the word "lifeless" instead, and it became instantly clear that it was the right choice. Not only did it allow us a bit more melodic interest, but in terms of its poetry, it captured better, more vividly, and with a greater variety of definition the significance of our savior, dying and deceased on the cross, and the way in which the faithful celebrate that day of the Triduum. Consider, in a hypothetical moment in a Good Friday preaching, the difference between using the word "dead" and the word "lifeless." It certainly may be that "dead" would be exactly the right word in a certain context. What would the word "lifeless" be able to bring to that same moment, though? Might it be a better choice most of the time?

Poetry, of course, is more than just choosing the right individual word, though as Mark Twain famously observed, "The difference between the almost right word and the right word is really a large matter—it's the difference between the lightning bug and the lightning." Poetry is stringing together many "right words" by use of various techniques to affect the sound of the text when read or sung aloud, to juxtapose various meanings and images, to create metaphor and synecdoche, and to utilize many other techniques to create a profundity of meaning that is—and where have we heard this before?—greater than the sum of its parts and in fact incapable of being expressed any other way. This is why poetry is the right (and perhaps only) linguistic vehicle capable of addressing core Christian beliefs like the paschal mystery, whether it be in song, poetry, catechesis, preaching, or ordinary conversations.

Many of us will easily recall the poem written and performed by Amanda Gorman at the 2021 presidential inauguration, "The Hill We Climb," and how her words spoke so eloquently and meaningfully to that moment of time in what some would rightly call a nearly religious or liturgical way. To address the topics that she did but with some sort of technical prose would not have brought about the unique moment in time that her poem created. Had her poem not been read aloud, not been performed but rather been read silently, here too the distinctive moment would have been lost. Poetry, particularly poetry read aloud or sung, speaks to the heart in ways most other language cannot.

Gorman's "The Hill We Climb," musically and poetically, is a master class in composition and presentation. Compositionally, it so well knew its context, its place in time and space: a time of division, racial inequity, global pandemic, insurrection—and the dawning, at least potentially, of a new day. Light and hope poetically oppose darkness and fear throughout; techniques like anaphora, enjambment, and allusion create rhythm and structure as well as a world that people recognize without needing it to be clearly described. Even in free verse, the internal rhymes and inbreaking of cadence give the listener moments to cling to, to remember, to repeat.

Her presentation of it embodied all these elements and through musical elements already discussed: varied thoughtful pauses, and higher- and lower-pitched speaking voices. There was even a physicality that extended down to her fingertips, at times almost dancing to the poetry she was reciting. This element of the moment is often overlooked in critical analyses one encounters.

"The Hill We Climb" was obviously well crafted and was presented for and in a particular moment. Those who create preaching would do well to consider their particular context of time and space when creating their reflections. The best liturgical music seems to be universal in terms of meeting a person at prayer where they are, no matter the context, just like Christ met those seeking miraculous healings. Yet it is a known fact in the realm of liturgical music that the best compositions come when someone is writing for a particular moment, a particular family of faith, filling a particular need. Writing hymns today, especially ones that might be published, can be an exacting challenge, as the writer needs to attend both to the local community vis-à-vis *lex orandi, lex credendi* (see chapter eight) and to the desire of the teaching authority of the Church to ensure the beliefs espoused in the hymn are constant and true.

When "Catholic Hymnody at the Service of the Church," from the US Conference of Catholic Bishops' Committee on Doctrine, appeared in December 2020 along with an accompanying memo that detailed the document's audiences and purposes, many in the world of liturgical music saw it, optimistically, as an opportunity to enter into dialogue with our bishops, an occasion where helpful distinctions might be made and mutually beneficial progress could be achieved.

The document, in broad strokes, concerns itself with an ostensible trend of incompleteness and imprecision in hymn texts, listing six "categories of potential deficiencies" as a way to evaluate their suitability for liturgy. Some specifically mentioned in the document as deficient include Marty Haugen's "All Are Welcome," Bob Hurd's "Led by the Spirit," and Bernadette Farrell's "God, Beyond All Names."

Our liturgical hymns should not—of course—communicate something antithetical to the faith. It should be obvious that our hymnals contain nothing of this ilk! This is not to say there cannot be legitimate concerns with some hymn texts. We must note, however, that new hymn texts are, in large part, created by persons with immense education, formation, spirituality, and talent. Texts are then further scrutinized and shaped by a team of editors equally qualified and talented before ever being put before a bishop for an imprimatur. All this takes place before these words find their way to the lips of the faithful at liturgy.

My worry is that the difficult task of evaluating and interpreting these poetic texts, or erroneously interpreting them too literally, has led some to judge them as inadequate. Frequently, they are beautiful, faithful, and, especially through the use of synecdoche, more truthful than two or three times the number of words is capable of being.

Poetry about the divine is challenging, but it is also an opportunity. An essay written with thousands of words and clear intelligibility is still inadequate to impart fully the ineffable divine; here, poetry and music at the service of the faith are invaluable. With fewer words and with symbolic language—and amplified by lovely melodies and harmonies—sacred poetry can create, between composer and singer, between singer and God, an ephemeral dialogue that allows for communication of intense and otherwise inexpressible beauty and truth.

Poetic texts by definition cannot say everything with complete and total precision, nor would we want them to. Singing whole chapters of the catechism verbatim, for instance, would quickly become particularly tedious. Could a demand be put forth, if one sets the Beatitudes to music, that all of them must be included in the first verse of a piece, lest a music director end a hymn "early" and render incomplete Christ's important teaching?

As someone educated by Dominicans, I am fond of distinctions. But some distinctions take far too long to explain and require so many nuances that the helpfulness of the distinction itself comes into question. The section of "Catholic Hymnody" that explains when the words "bread" or "bread of life" are and are not suitable reads to my eyes in just this way. There is such a thing as a distinction without difference. Specifically regarding "All Are Welcome," a wise theologian friend of mine, Harold Velazquez, observes that "the banquet *isn't* presented as ordinary; the context *does* help us interpret bread and wine as synecdoche; 'let us build a house' need not be interpreted as being in conflict with the work of the Trinity in building the Church."

The same section of "Catholic Hymnody" also observes that many current eucharistic hymn texts utilize only vocabulary that regards Communion as "table fellowship" and excludes sacrificial language. On the surface this seems an accurate assessment. Consider, though, this text from the Missal itself, a prayer after Communion from Wednesday of the Third Week of Lent: "May the heavenly banquet, at which we have been fed, / sanctify us, O Lord, / and, cleansing us of all errors, / make us worthy of your promises from on high. / Through Christ our Lord." Is this prayer speaking of Communion exclusively as a banquet? Or should we, by noting the language of sanctification and cleansing, also infer its sacrificial elements? *Lex orandi, lex credendi*, after all.

Poetry is hard. It is hard to create, and it is hard to interpret. What is theologically important regarding Communion, ultimately, is that it is both sacrifice and banquet simultaneously, a memorial meal at which Christ is made manifest before us as saving victim and is consumed to sustain us spiritually. If the prayer above communicates all of this, then the phrase "the feast that frees us" in Marty Haugen's hymn "All Are Welcome" must be seen as one of the most concise, beautiful, and truthful phrases of poetry in all our hymnals.

How could we not want the words of our homilies, by utilizing the poetic language of most effective and good modern hymnody, to achieve similar effects? How could we not desire our day-to-day interactions to embody these beautiful truths by allowing music, liturgy, and The Word to dwell richly in relationship with each other and bear tangible fruit as they impact all we say and do?

Simultaneously, as careful as we might be in choosing words and delivering them effectively, we can also note that hymn texts often can be sung to different familiar hymn tunes. The comical example of this is that one can sing the words of "Amazing Grace" to the melody of the theme song of *Gilligan's Island* (or vice versa, of course). Sometimes the choice of a hymn tune can profoundly impact the way the hymn text paired with it is sung or heard. And sometimes the choice of a tune can have an impact we can't imagine and certainly don't even expect.

Early in my career, for a Christmas Eve mass, I chose to sing "O Little Town of Bethlehem," but not to the familiar American tune (ST. LOUIS). I picked instead the British tune for the same words (FOREST GREEN)—to this day I'm not sure exactly why, other than I do like the sturdiness and contours of that Vaughan Williams tune. After mass, a young man came up to speak with me, and specifically to thank me. He explained that he was originally from South Africa but was spending the Christmas holiday in the States for the first time in his life to be with his American fiancé. Though being with his love was wonderful, he had found being far from home, far from the familiar, a bit depressing. But then, when we began singing this hymn during mass, everything changed. His American fiancé looked up, puzzled, and said, "Wait, that's not 'O Little Town of Bethlehem,'" to which he replied excitedly, "Oh yes it is! Oh yes it is!" as that was the tune familiar to him from his childhood overseas. My spurious choice of a piece of music was the best Christmas gift I perhaps ever gave anyone. It helped that young man truly recognize and celebrate The Word Incarnate that year. Even our unconscious choices, be they musical or textual, can have profound impacts, sometimes more so than our careful and deliberate ones.

10

Exploring the Relationship between Music, Liturgy, and The Word

Silence

But enough for the moment on speech and music—what about silences? Recall that CSL 30 demands silence in the liturgy too. Scripture time and time again reveals silence as the principal place God speaks to the faithful: in a whispering wind, in stillness, in the quiet time set apart from the cares of the world.

Silence is a valuable and, I dare say, underused facet of music. Often, there is more music made in a moment or two of rests than in hundreds of notes surrounding that silence. Particularly, silences—rests—can give a singer a moment to contemplate the meaning and power of the profound poetry just sung, without the worry of finding either the next pitch or the next lyric. What good is it to sing the most amazing text if we aren't given time to ponder it and allow it to truly rest on our hearts? I find, for instance, that recent settings of the Gloria are guilty of racing through the text, trying first and foremost to meet the goal of "getting through" the liturgical hymn as quickly as possible. Doing so does a great disservice to this ancient hymn of praise.

Silence is also a critical component of the Dominican method of seeking truth—to listen for understanding, one, of course, must be silent; that should go without saying. The listening, though, goes beyond just comprehension. Recall this line from the earlier story of Dominic and the innkeeper: "Dominic listened attentively: he didn't just hear his host out, nor did he judge him, but rather showed his openness to him." Some tellings of the story indicate that Dominic stayed up all night, just listening to the innkeeper's many complaints about the Church before he offered a single word into the conversation. The silence of true listening is more than the absence of sounds; it is attention, openness; it is *agape*; it is Christ. Silence is where God is, where God speaks.

Similarly, with preaching, we must not feel compelled to fill every little moment with the sound of our voice or rush through what we have prepared. In fact, it can be quite powerful indeed to intentionally place silence within our preaching, to make the silence an event of its own. Silence, especially unexpected silence, doesn't just give the assembly a chance to contemplate the preaching up to that moment; it can also draw them in and invite them to engage more deeply with what is to come. Silence is a perfect breeding ground for anticipation and curiosity.

Silence within the liturgy overall, Pope Francis reminds us, also belongs to the Holy Spirit: "[S]ilence is not an inner haven in which to hide oneself in some sort of intimate isolation, as if leaving the ritual form behind as a distraction. That kind of silence would contradict the essence itself of the celebration. Liturgical silence is something much more grand: it is a symbol of the presence and action of the Holy Spirit who animates the entire action of the celebration" (*Desiderio Desideravi* 52).

Several years ago, I began serving as an accompanist at a Jewish synagogue, Congregation Shaare Emeth in suburban St. Louis, following a curious chain of events. There isn't space here for the whole saga of how that came to be, but briefly, I had hired a cantor at the Catholic shrine I was working at, Scott, who was (and is) Jewish. Scott began also singing at Shaare Emeth while they were between Cantors (capital *C*). Their longtime accompanist then left his post, and the head rabbi there asked Scott if he knew of anyone who could play the sorts of newer music they had begun using; he recommended me, and I soon after met with a member of the congregation, Ron, for an audition and interview. During our meeting, Ron asked me if I knew "Lift Up Your Hearts" by Roc O'Connor and could play it. Ron, I soon found out, was (and is) an organist and had been recruited to play at a Catholic church down the road during his college days, just as the music of the St. Louis Jesuits was exploding across the nation. I still play at Shaare Emeth regularly, and the experiences there of music and worship never cease to invigorate me as I compare and contrast the styles, the theologies, the shared texts and their uses, and the common Adonai we worship.

I bring this facet of my life into the conversation now for two reasons. Firstly, each service I play for at Shaare Emeth includes a length of congregational silent prayer. The silence is communal, but the prayers of that moment of worship are, of course, quite singular. This is one of the main gifts of silence: it can allow for prayer that is simultaneously corporate and individual. Within our worship, especially within preaching, the silence allows for each congregant to take the fodder of what has just been presented to them, dwell more deeply with it, and take it to relational communication directly with the divine. At Eucharist, the presidential prayers begin with "Let us pray," yet many presiders don't actually give their assemblies time to do so! The presidential prayers are also called "collects" because that is, in part, their function: to collect the silent prayers of the assembly into one presidential prayer offered to God.

Just as the silences within a piece of music give the performers or listeners a moment's pause to collect themselves, briefly take stock of the sounds and harmonies that have just preceded, and prepare for what may come next, so too pauses in worship and preaching allow our spiritual sensibilities to do the same. At Shaare Emeth, the time of silent prayer is brought to a close typically by singing a setting of these words from Psalm 19:

> *Yih'yu l'ratzon imrei fi,*
> *V'hegyon libi l'fanecha*
> *Adonai, tzuri, v'goali.*

יִהְיוּ לְרָצוֹן אִמְרֵי פִי

וְהֶגְיוֹן לִבִּי לְפָנֶיךָ,

יהוה צוּרִי וְגֹאֲלִי.

May the words of my mouth and the meditations of my heart
be acceptable to you,
Adonai, my Rock and my Redeemer.

The second reason I bring my experiences of worship at Shaare
Emeth into these writings is to share one particular prayer that is
a part of evening services from time to time. It is a small poem,
part of chapter seven of *The Sabbath* by Abraham Joshua Heschel:
"Eternity Utters a Day." Here is the text:

A thought has blown the market place away.
There is a song in the wind and joy in the trees.
The Sabbath arrives in the world,
scattering a song in the silence of the night: eternity utters a day.[1]

It's such a perfect bit of profundity encapsulated in so few words. I
have for some time now adored the musical setting that we use to
accompany these words, by composer Dan Nichols. I have known
for a while that he had adapted the text slightly (substituting in
shabbat for "The Sabbath") in his setting, but I more recently discovered that he (and those who created the current prayer book
used at Shaare Emeth) also clipped a final line off of the text:

Where are the words that could compete with such might?

Where indeed! The thought, the divine idea of the Sabbath, brings
our stirrings to rest, gives music and delight to our lives, and breaks
through "the silence of the night." Who are we to even presume
our words have any such power? God speaks, is always speaking,

but too often human "noise pollution" keeps us from hearing it, much like light pollution keeps those of us who dwell in urban settings from seeing as much of the night sky as those who live in the broad open spaces of ranch country, for instance, where no human-made light exists for miles and miles. Do our own lights keep us from seeing the divine light? Let us pray, perhaps, not for light, but instead for darkness, for silence, so that we may become more aware of God's light, God's voice.

It must be noted, before continuing, that there is in fact no such thing as complete silence, at least for living humans. Even in an anechoic chamber, a soundproofed room designed so the walls, ceiling, and floor absorb all sounds (and keep them from echoing), there are still sounds to be heard. John Cage, the experimental twentieth-century composer famed for his composition *4'33"*, visited one once and talked about the experience this way: "I heard two sounds, one high and one low. When I described them to the engineer in charge, he informed me that the high one was my nervous system in operation, the low one my blood in circulation."[2] Even in absolute silence, the glory and the pinnacle of God's creation is still producing sound, sounds still heard by the same creation that is making them. Cage would not say it this way, but his composition, which puts the listener into four minutes and thirty-three seconds of "silence" in its own way, is a sort of revelation of God and of the creative gifts God gave humanity, including music and all other noises one might hear. Cage once performed the piece himself in the middle of Harvard Square, where one could hear traffic, the subway, other street performers, audience reactions, and so much more—all the sounds of human life and activity that God has given us the gifts to create. Silence here sonically paints the truest significance of the Eternal Logos, The Word of Creation, still active and alive in each of us today.

Silence may also be used by more conventional composers as a more specific bit of "text painting," a particular technique that music has at its disposal to amplify the meaning of the particular words it is setting. "But," I hear you ask, "how can silence expand on the meaning of a word or two if by definition there is no sung word able to be paired with a moment of silence?"

We turn to a setting of Psalm 137, the lament of a people exiled from their homeland (example 8 in the appendix). The refrain includes the word "silenced," we can see. Here, the music I've written for this bit of text includes three beats of vocal rests following "silenced"—but only because, as noted, I could not pair silence itself with any vocal sound. Consider how the feeling and significance of the text would change with those rests omitted—how odd it would be to sing about our own tongues being silenced and then not include any silence at all! Here, the singer (and listener, if that is the case) is given time to contemplate what life might be like with all speech and singing muted and why the original psalmist, far from home, contemplated that too.

Consider the more secular uses of silence. A moment of silence is frequently introduced at various gatherings in remembrance of lives lost. What words would instead be more expressive? Truly, none would. Often, civic protesters use the contrast of silence to more effectively make their point and their presence known. Truth, after all, isn't made any more "truthy" because it is loud. A parent, finding themself upset at the behavior of a child, might suddenly become much more quiet or completely silent in expressing their frustration and disappointment. In any of these moments, the Gospel is preached not through words but through silent action, recalling the apocryphal admonition from St. Francis already mentioned in these pages.

For my money, one of the greatest Christian truths is revealed in one particular stretch of silence—not only silence, really, but also inactivity, not just for a moment but for a whole twenty-four-hour period of time. Christian author Max Lucado says this about Holy Saturday, the day (sunset to sunset) between Good Friday and Easter Sunday:

> Jesus is silent on Saturday. The women have anointed his
> body and placed it in Joseph's tomb. The cadaver of Christ
> is as mute as the stone which guards it. He spoke much on

Friday. He will liberate the slaves of death on Sunday. But on Saturday, Jesus is silent.

So is God. He made himself heard on Friday. He tore the curtains of the temple, opened the graves of the dead, rocked the earth, blocked the sun of the sky, and sacrificed the Son of Heaven. Earth heard much of God on Friday.

Nothing on Saturday. Jesus is silent. God is silent. Saturday is silent.[3]

Consider that one of the most powerful expressions of who God is, who we are, and what and who we are called to be is found each year in this subdued and quiet Saturday. Perhaps our efforts at sharing The Word can learn from this facet of our faith and our God, too.

To that end, here's another liturgical preaching example as a witness to and focusing on the power of both poetic language and silence within preaching. You will note that most of the poetic language in it isn't created by the homilist but by the great American poet Emily Dickinson. Perhaps you don't have the gift of creating beautiful poetic language yourself, and there is no shame in that. You do know, though, many people, perhaps some who sit in your very pews each Sunday, who do have that gift, I am sure! Seek out those gifts and use them.

Preaching example—use of poetic language and silence:
"And Jesus Wept"

Preaching on John 11:1-45—The Raising of Lazarus
Catholic Lectionary, Cycle A, Fifth Sunday of Lent [34]

It's perhaps best known as an answer to a trivia question: What is the shortest Bible verse? Do you know which it is?

[Intentional five-second pause]

It's found in this Sunday's gospel reading: "And Jesus wept." People who reflect and preach on the pericope of the raising of Lazarus often rightly point to this verse as indicative of Jesus's humanity. Even the crowd that has gathered that day remark on the love that Jesus must have felt for his friend.

But do they miss what's really going on? Do we?

[Intentional five-second pause]

Jesus has just encountered Mary, the sister of Lazarus, and other Jews who had come to mourn with her. The passage says Jesus is "perturbed" and "deeply troubled" at seeing them. He asks to visit the tomb and then weeps.

Certainly, this passage is about many things—the resurrection foreshadowed, messianic power, and the divinity and humanity of Jesus Christ, to name a few. But when someone identifies the weeping of Jesus as evidence of his humanity, as evidence that he shared our human experiences completely except our sinfulness, that's where I think something important is overlooked.

I do believe Jesus was despondent at his friend's death—though he also seems to delay his trip to visit his at-that-time ill friend on purpose, and he seems to know before he departs to make the journey that Lazarus has already died. What is it, then, that brings Jesus to tears?

[Intentional five-second pause]

I believe it's empathy: empathy at witnessing Lazarus's sister's and the others' mourning—seeing and hearing their tears and grief. Empathy: the ability to understand and share in the feelings of someone else. While there are more and more scientific studies that suggest certain animals show, for instance, consolation, there is no doubt that humans by far are the most capable of empathy.

It's so important that Jesus experienced empathy. God chose for our salvation to become like us in almost every way, and Jesus would not have been fully human without it. We are not fully human without it, and yet this human experience seems so sorely lacking in the modern world.

Emily Dickinson, the famed American poet, seems to have been no stranger to grief. Her poem "I Measure Every Grief I Meet"[4] seems to also wonder if her grief will find any empathy in those around her, if anyone may know and understand her sadness and pain through the sadness and pain of their own:

> I measure every Grief I meet
> With narrow, probing, eyes–
> I wonder if It weighs like Mine–
> Or has an Easier size.
>
> I wonder if They bore it long–
> Or did it just begin–
> I could not tell the Date of Mine–
> It feels so old a pain–
>
> I wonder if it hurts to live–
> And if They have to try–
> And whether–could They choose between–
> It would not be–to die–
>
> I note that Some–gone patient long–
> At length, renew their smile–
> An imitation of a Light
> That has so little Oil–

I wonder if when Years have piled–
Some Thousands–on the Harm–
That hurt them early–such a lapse
Could give them any Balm–

Or would they go on aching still
Through Centuries of Nerve–
Enlightened to a larger Pain–
In Contrast with the Love–

The Grieved–are many–I am told–
There is the various Cause–
Death–is but one–and comes but once–
And only nails the eyes–

There's Grief of Want–and grief of Cold–
A sort they call "Despair"–
There's Banishment from native Eyes–
In sight of Native Air–

And though I may not guess the kind–
Correctly–yet to me
A piercing Comfort it affords
In passing Calvary–

To note the fashions–of the Cross–
And how they're mostly worn–
Still fascinated to presume
That Some–are like my own–

[Intentional fifteen-second pause]

Today, Jesus of Calvary, Jesus of the cross, calls us again to empathy: to understand the plight of refugees fleeing war and destruction *[brief pause]*, to sense the anxiety of those whose healthcare is more expensive than they can afford *[brief pause]*, to feel the hunger of someone who depends on the kindness of others every day for their daily bread *[brief pause]*, or simply to share the sadness of someone who has lost a loved one or is having a bad day or just needs someone to listen to their frustrations.

"And Jesus wept." It's more than just trivia—it's an important part of who we are and who Jesus was and is, and it's our connection to something truly divine.

[Pause for at least two minutes of silent reflection.]

11

Including Music in Preaching and Sharing The Word

Allow me to include a brief note for this extensive study on the practice of including music itself—singing—during liturgical preaching. I suspect we've all experienced this before, whether it was the preacher, the music ministry, or the entire assembly who sang. We've probably experienced wonderful examples of this—and excruciatingly poor ones as well. What aspects of trying this technique can make it either so very good or so very bad?

On one level, it's not so different from including a poem into the preaching, as was done in the example at the end of the previous chapter; it just happens that the poem would be sung instead of spoken and would quite possibly include someone's assistance beyond the preacher themself (and needing that assistance is itself a double-edged sword). To make the inclusion of music into a homily successful, here are a few tips to consider:

- First, the inclusion of music must be planned and practiced and not done on a spur of the moment whim. Otherwise, lyrics will be forgotten, singers will start in a key too high or too low, the accompanists will be left wondering if they missed a memo, and on and on and on.

- This is not to say that there is no room at all for spontaneity—there is no controlling the Holy Spirit, after all. Perhaps preachers and musicians should have a more general chat about expectations should there be a chance the Spirit will inspire one or the other at some upcoming service.

- Ensure that the text, as with any poetry used, is indeed precisely connected to the rest of the preaching's content. This helps the music become a powerful memory in the minds and souls of the assembly and not distract from a more important point.

- Music is especially effective if it's (1) a short phrase used throughout the homily, (2) a larger portion of a piece used to end the homily, or (3) both. But be careful not to be too repetitive; a little seasoning like this goes a long way.

- If the music that is part of the preaching is used again later in the mass or service, perhaps as a concluding hymn after some amount of time has passed, such useful repetition will help your congregation better retain and live that message outside the church doors.

What about preaching on the text of a piece of liturgical music? We are accustomed to preaching that breaks open the word of God, as CSL instructs preachers to do. We also know that, in practice, other sources are frequently utilized for homilies, either held alongside the scriptures in order to develop new insights or, sometimes, as primary source material themselves. Some of these materials will include poetry, as we have already seen, as well as other Church writings, writings of the saints, current spiritual reflections from any number of theologians, and sometimes even humor. Music, especially liturgical music, could easily be a source of preaching fodder as well, either to be held alongside scripture or as primary material.

Even secular music, in this regard, is not without value. Some years ago, a woman named Anna Scally had a quite successful youth ministry as a DJ for dances at religious youth events—rallies and the like. She had a gift for identifying in the secular popular music of the time religious themes and insights that could be shared with young people enjoying their time together in community. If we can perceive with "God's ears," as it were, these elements of faith are still apparent in popular music today. Identifying these elements is not always the easiest pursuit however, and there are some traps and pitfalls to be wary of.

Consider Pharrell Williams's 2013 hit song "Happy." I was speaking about this song with some adults at a religious youth event one afternoon when one remarked how much, from a faith perspective, they appreciated the line in the song "Clap along if you feel like happiness is the truth." Following the Dominican model, I inquired with a question that, really, wasn't so innocent. Rather, it was one of those questions intended to lead the receiver to the same conclusion I had already reached: "Do you like that line in the song because the truth ought to make us happy or because whatever makes us happy is in fact the truth?" After a moment of pondering, my conversation partner realized the potential trap in that particular line, that it didn't exactly say what she thought it did at first. (Recall that writing and interpreting poetry is a fiendishly difficult task!)

On perhaps safer ground, often our liturgical music is scriptural, at least paraphrasing scripture if not using it verbatim, and we have already observed that music allows any given text to take up residence in a person's soul much more easily than the same words without music attached. We can also observe that the liturgy could be described as "over-texted"—and that, along with silence, fewer words are likely better than more. Perhaps our preaching, relying from time to time on sacred music, could utilize fewer words more effectively. More words, as I noted at the beginning of this book, do not make something more memorable or more profound. What we need more of in the liturgy, frankly, is more contemplation, more mystery, and more silence—as also already noted.

Additionally, we have already, earlier in this chapter, observed that music shared within a homily can be especially effective if that music is later repeated. That effectiveness becomes more profound if the text of the piece is preached upon, is broken open and directly connected to the assembly's everyday living. If the preaching does this successfully, then when the music is later brought to life on the assembly's lips, one will achieve not only memorable repetition but an embodiment of living faith by active participation, an embodiment that has a real chance of continuing to blossom and grow once the communal prayer is complete and the faithful go forth to their homes, neighborhoods, and workplaces.

Further, realistically speaking, the music for a particular liturgy is typically planned and rehearsed long before a homily for that same liturgy is prepared and written. If the expectation is that the two elements, music and preaching, are at least working cooperatively, if not symbiotically, it is much more possible for the homilist to check what the liturgical music will be for the coming weekend than for the music director to check weeks and months ahead of time what a homily will be about so that appropriate music can be planned.

Another practical point here for preachers who find it a challenge every week, if not several times each week, to prepare meaningful and engaging texts to share with their congregation: it is far, far easier—not to mention likely more meaningful and much closer to what a homily is meant to be—to preach with poetry and symbolism rather than with words of doctrine or catechesis. Of course, we must address both from time to time and occasionally even preach directly on doctrine or catechetical material. A call for more poetry and symbolism also doesn't mean that the preaching cannot directly speak to issues of the current time, like social justice, human dignity, and the like. I hope the preaching examples in previous chapters show, rather, that an approach that emphasizes the what and why of the mysteries of our faith is better suited for this than an approach that emphasizes the how.

Remember: mysteries don't mix well with "how" language, nor should they be expected to. They are mysteries, after all; why can't we let them remain so? I earlier mentioned that much—though not all—of society today has, rightly, a nearly incontrovertible relationship with science and, to a point, the scientific method; everything must have a cause and effect and be able to be studied, tangibly observed, and proven, one way or another. There is, notably, a large difference between proving that God exists and believing in God through signs. The how of who God is, to a believer, ought to be far less relevant than the what and why of who God is.

That our faith is built upon supernatural mystery means it is often best to use musical, poetic language to speak of it, to pray within it, to seek to grow in unity with all believers of it. In expounding upon the mysteries of the faith, as preachers are called to do, it is far easier to preach on the poetry and symbolism of the Trinity than to explain the doctrine of it; it is far easier to preach the poetry and symbolism of the resurrection than to explain how it happened; it is far easier to preach on the poetry and symbolism of Eucharist than on how it is confected:

> The myst'ry of your presence, Lord,
> No mortal tongue can tell:
> Whom all the world cannot contain
> Comes in our hearts to dwell.
> ("Gift of Finest Wheat"[1])

Our faith is one of mystery, paradox, the supernatural—things unseen but believed. Music, and the poetry in relationship with it, operates most successfully on the level of symbolism and is therefore perhaps best suited for expressing and making this faith real, tangible, vital, and transformative. Still, "Every symbol is at the same time both powerful and fragile," Pope Francis reminds us in *Desiderio Desideravi* (44). We must take care to use them, as disciples and evangelists, carefully, pastorally, and with intention. Can our preaching do this? Can our day-to-day living? I certainly believe both can, and I hope you do as well. Can our preaching and living The Word learn from liturgical music and become even more successful in helping the faithful pray, live, and grow in unity with one another and with God? I believe that they can and that they must—the stakes are rather high.

12

Why Explore the Relationship between Music, Liturgy, and The Word

Practical Considerations

This book began with an exploration of the scriptural, traditional, and liturgical reasons to explore the relationship between music, liturgy, and The Word, and of what each could learn from the others to enhance our preaching and our living the faith. If that was not enough to convince one to pursue such a study, there are some very practical reasons right now that we must give attention to these matters, foremost among them the shrinking, diminishing Church, at least in America (and "the West" as a whole).

Our current moment is a time when we need to be working hard—not only to invite and welcome the faithful back to church following the COVID-19 pandemic but also to retain our assemblies and grow for the future. As much as the Church on one level is immutable, the Church is also always changing, and we as ministers must be willing to change with it when it makes sense to. As such, an emphasis on good, engaging, and effective preaching that adapts to the current moment is particularly necessary. We are at a time where aspects of social justice, mercy, and community are at the fore of society and Church, eclipsing in part an emphasis on rules, doctrine, and dogma. Yet, ultimately, all of these facets of our faith should and must work together. The brief preaching examples included in the previous chapters of this book, I hope, stand as positive examples in this regard.

And how do we know that good, engaging, and effective preaching is particularly necessary for growing our assemblies and retaining church membership? Studies show us this quite clearly:

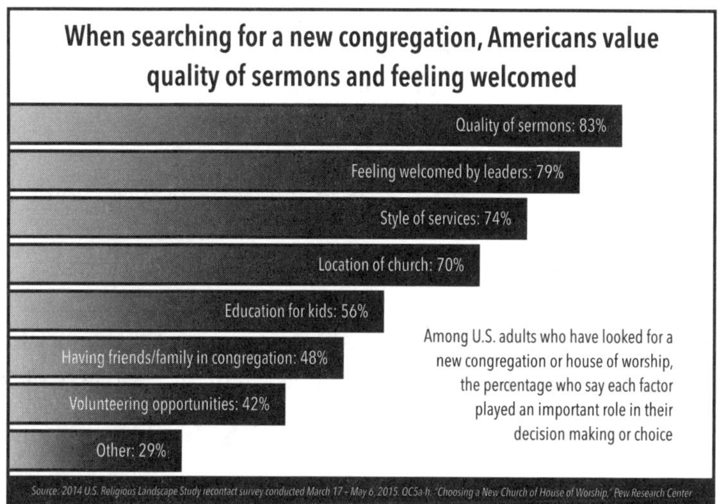

This Pew Research Center study from August 2016 learned that when Christian adults in the United States are looking for a new congregation, 83 percent of them value the quality of sermons as an important factor in their choice, more than any other attribute asked about. That's 7 out of 8 adults who list the preaching as an important factor—more than the style of services or the location of the churches.

Further, the US Conference of Catholic Bishops document Sing to the Lord details the overall effect that liturgy, as font and apex, has on the whole of the Christian people and the whole of the Christian life:

> Obedient to Christ and to the Church, we gather in liturgical assembly, week after week. As our predecessors did, we find ourselves "singing psalms, hymns and spiritual songs with

gratitude in [our] hearts to God." This common, sung expression of faith within liturgical celebrations strengthens our faith when it grows weak and draws us into the divinely inspired voice of the Church at prayer. Faith grows when it is well expressed in celebration. *Good celebrations can foster and nourish faith. Poor celebrations may weaken it.* Good music "make[s] the liturgical prayers of the Christian community more alive and fervent so that everyone can praise and beseech the Triune God more powerfully, more intently and more effectively." (STTL 5; emphasis added)

The emphasized text above bears repeating: "Good celebrations can foster and nourish faith. Poor celebrations may weaken it." While STTL is, of course, a document about liturgical music, we can also quickly see how the care and attention given to preaching is just as important in the creation of effective and prayerful liturgies. One could even adapt that last sentence above, which was initially drawn from Pius XII's 1955 encyclical *Musicae Sacrae* (On Sacred Music), and point it just as easily toward preaching: Good *preaching* "make[s] the liturgical prayers of the Christian community more alive and fervent so that everyone can praise and beseech the Triune God more powerfully, more intently and more effectively."

The 2015 *Homiletic Directory* (36), drawing from several other sources, states the importance the homily has to the life of the Church—our missions of discipleship, evangelization, and service—in this way:

> Pope Benedict XVI added a coda to the traditional fourfold process of *lectio divina*: "We do well also to remember that the process of lectio divina is not concluded until it arrives at action (*actio*), which moves the believer to make his or her life a gift for others in charity" (VD 87). Viewed in its liturgical context, this suggests the "missa," the sending out of God's people who have been instructed by God's Word and nourished by their participation in the Paschal Mystery through the Eucharist. It is significant that the Exhortation *Verbum*

Domini concludes with a lengthy consideration of the Word of God in the world; preaching, when combined with the nourishment of the sacraments received in faith, opens up the members of the liturgical assembly to practical expressions of charity. Similarly, citing Pope John Paul II's teaching that "communion and mission are profoundly interconnected" (*Christifideles laici* 32), Pope Francis exhorts all believers:

> In fidelity to the example of the Master, it is vitally important for the Church today to go forth and preach the Gospel to all: to all places, on all occasions, without hesitation, reluctance or fear. The joy of the Gospel is for all people: no one can be excluded (EG [*Evangelii Gaudium*] 23).

We may realize, intellectually, that liturgy is the font and apex of the Christian life, but how do we make that lofty notion a reality for the faithful? We create liturgical music and preaching that more than work in tandem—they grow and flourish together. This, in turn, emboldens the assembly to live that interrelationship between music and preaching in the interrelationship of the liturgy and their very lives and to recognize the cooperation and common purpose that all liturgical components share, all within a liturgy that has an innate integrity and a wholeness of purpose.

None of this is of any worth, of course, if people are not drawn to worship in the first place. In 2021, a Gallup poll showed that fewer than half of Americans, 47 percent, belonged to a church, synagogue, or mosque. This is the first time the percentage has dropped below 50 percent in more than 80 years. The Catholic Church saw the greatest decline over the last 20 years, dropping 18 percent. The "Rise of the Nones" is no longer able to be denied—"Nones" are, in fact, a majority.[1]

And we might be surprised at when people, on average, leave the Catholic faith. A two-year study from the Center for Applied Research in the Apostolate (CARA) released in 2018 found that, of those who left the Catholic Church, the median age for doing so was 13 years old. Thirteen! Further, 74 percent of the 214 former Catholics interviewed said that they had decided to leave the

Church between the ages of 10 and 20.[2] Time truly is of the essence here, in so many ways.

"Today this scripture passage is fulfilled in your hearing" (Luke 4:21), Jesus preached—or should I say *challenged*—at the beginning of his public ministry. Pope Francis, after mass on the Sunday of the Word of God in 2022, addressed the crowd gathered for the midday *Angelus* prayer. This passage from Luke had been part of the gospel reading at that earlier mass. He told the faithful,

> The Word of God is always "today." It begins with a "today;" when you read the Word of God, a "today" begins in your soul, if you understand it well. It is not like ancient history, no. Today, it speaks to your heart.
>
> Sometimes it happens that our sermons and our teachings remain generic, abstract; they do not touch the soul and the life of the people. Yes, at times one hears impeccable conferences, well-constructed speeches, but they do not move the heart and so everything remains as before.
>
> If those who preach want to give lectures or conferences, let them do so but elsewhere; not at the time of the homily, where they must give the Word in a way that rouses hearts.[3]

The liturgy should form us, shape us, send us out with missionary purpose to grow the Church and bring all to Christ and salvation. We've explored how sharing The Word outside of church can be molded by lived *agape*, sacrificial and covenantal love. Does our sharing of The Word reveal that essential facet—creating, sanctifying, redeeming—of the Trinity? Do our creative actions give glory to God or to ourselves? Do our efforts at bringing forth communion and community bring all to greater holiness, or are some left out? Does the way we share God's redemption with others encompass both mercy and justice, both accountability and restoration? The sharing of The Word inside the church doors—through scripture, preaching, and music—must be the same sharing of The Word outside the church doors—through thoughts, words, and deeds. *Lex orandi, lex credendi—lex vivendi.*

If we invite someone to worship, will they experience inside the church doors what they know of church from the other aspects of their lives? There must be an innate integrity and a wholeness of purpose—not just within liturgy but infused into the whole of the Christian life. Without that, any invitation we might give to someone will be seen for what it is: hollow, insincere, perhaps even worthless.

The truth—the Truth—that is at the core of this integrity and wholeness cannot be found by intentionally creating and furthering divisions. It cannot be found in derision or pursuit of victory that also creates losers. It cannot be found in mercy without justice or in justice without mercy. It cannot be found at all outside of communion, community, and conversation. These need *agape*; these need a pursuit of truth that listens, understands, inquires, and distinguishes. These are not impossible things—or even hard things! They are, though, for most of us, quite different and will need practice and work, and our determination, diligence, and discipline.

Music here has been brought into conversation with the liturgy and The Word in an effort to make clearer the interconnectedness of these elements of our faith lives, and to show us a clearer and more fruitful path forward in allowing them to more fully express that same faith. The immediacy and urgency of this goal is apparent. Let us pray to the Holy Spirit for the willingness and the perseverance to meet the challenge:

> Come, Holy Spirit,
> with your light and your courage.
> Shine brightly on the path ahead,
> that we may see what it is we are called to do.
> Share your courage,
> that we may be emboldened to do it.
> Amen.

Epilogue

There is a hymn text that effortlessly illustrates everything I've tried to persuasively lay forth in this project: that preaching, living The Word, and liturgical music must share a strong relationship with one another for several reasons. Preaching, in particular, can and should learn from liturgical music several structures, techniques, and vocabularies, not only for the betterment of the preaching itself, but for the good of the whole Christian community.

The hymn "When in Our Music God Is Glorified" (example 9 in the appendix) embodies all this and more in five succinct verses, each ending with the acclamation of praise that is our song as Christians. Augustine of Hippo is often credited with saying, "We are an Easter people, and alleluia is our song!" As we heard in chapter three, that outburst of praise is multiplied, both sonically and spiritually, because it is sung. (In fact, our liturgical documents instruct us to omit the gospel acclamation if it is not sung.) This powerful and brief hymn shall have the last word of this endeavor. Let it instruct us and guide us as we seek to improve our liturgical efforts, as always, for the glorification of God and the sanctification of the people. Let it also be our fervent prayer, relational and communal, sincere and devout, as we strive to more faithfully live the Gospel in word and deed.

When in our music God is glorified,
And adoration leaves no room for pride,
It is as though the whole creation cried: Alleluia!

How often, making music, we have found
A new dimension in the world of sound,
As worship moved us to a more profound Alleluia!

So has the Church, in liturgy and song,
In faith and love, through centuries of wrong,
Borne witness to the truth in ev'ry tongue: Alleluia!

And did not Jesus sing a psalm that night
When utmost evil strove against the light?
Then let us sing, for whom he won the fight: Alleluia!

Let ev'ry instrument be tuned for praise!
Let all rejoice who have a voice to raise!
And may God give us faith to sing always: Alleluia![1]

APPENDIX

Musical Examples

Please visit https://litpress.org/incarnate-word-song to listen to the following musical examples.

Example 1

Celtic Alleluia

Example 2

"Amen" from *Mass of Creation*

Text: ICEL, © 2010
Music: *Mass of Creation*, Marty Haugen, © 1984, 1985, 2010, GIA Publications, Inc.

Example 3

This Is How

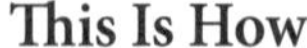

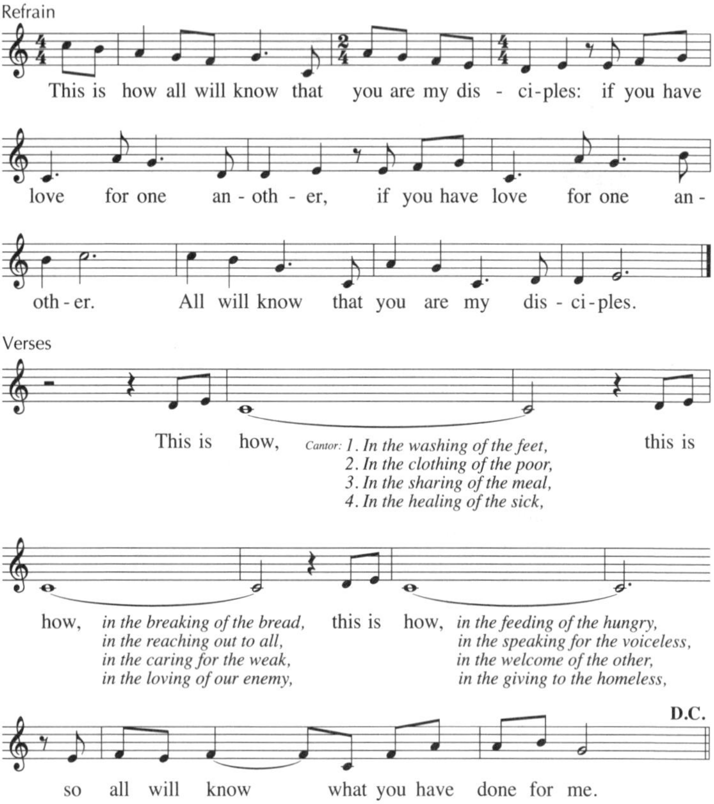

Text: Refrain, John 13:35; Chris de Silva, b.1967
Tune: Chris de Silva, b.1967

Example 4

Taste and See

Text: Psalm 34; James E. Moore, Jr., b.1951
Tune: James E. Moore, Jr., b.1951
© 1983, GIA Publications, Inc.

Example

The Cry of the Poor

Example 6

Alleluia! Alleluia

Text: 87 87 D; Christopher Wordsworth, 1807–1885, alt.
Music: HYMN TO JOY; Ludwig van Beethoven, 1770–1827; adapt. and harm. by Edward Hodges, 1796–1867.

Note: When guitar and keyboard play together, keyboardists should improvise using the guitar chords above the melody.

Example 7

I Give My Spirit

Based on Psalm 31

Words and Music by
Shannon Cerneka and Orin Johnson

Example 8

Psalm 137—Let My Tongue Be Silenced

for the musicians of the National Shrine of
Our Lady of the Snows, Belleville, Illinois

Orin Johnson
July 9-10, 2009

Example 9

When in Our Music God Is Glorified

Text: Fred Pratt Green, 1903–2000, © 1972, Hope Publishing Company
Tune: ENGELBERG, 10 10 10 with alleluia; Charles V. Stanford, 1852–1924

Notes

Introduction

1. Excerpts from Pope Francis, apostolic letter *Desiderio Desideravi*, June 29, 2022, © Libreria Editrice Vaticana. Used with permission.

Chapter 6

1. Kath, "Word of the Day—Homily," *For Reading Addicts*, accessed July 2, 2022, https://forreadingaddicts.co.uk/word-of-the-day/word-day-homily/20065.

2. Fr. Bruno Esposito, OP, "An Order Born in an Inn: The Dominicans," trans. Fr. Gregory Pearson, OP, Veritas, accessed July 2, 2022, https://www.padrebruno.com/an-order-born-in-an-inn-the-dominicans/. Used with permission.

Chapter 7

1. This story is, in fact, a true story from my childhood!

Chapter 10

1. Excerpt from THE SABBATH: ITS MEANING FOR MODERN MAN by Abraham Joshua Heschel. Copyright © 1951 by Abraham Joshua Heschel. Copyright renewed 1979 by Sylvia Heschel. Reprinted by permission of Farrar, Straus and Giroux. All Rights Reserved.

2. Excerpt from an address given at the Music Teachers National Association convention in 1957, *Loose Filter*, https://www.loosefilter.com/the_loose_filter_project_/2010/09/john-cage-quote-of-the-day-2-1.html.

3. Max Lucado, "The Silence of Saturday," accessed July 2, 2022, https://maxlucado.com/the-silence-of-saturday/. Used with permission.

4. THE POEMS OF EMILY DICKINSON, edited by Thomas H. Johnson, Cambridge, Mass.: The Belknap Press of Harvard University Press, Copyright © 1951, 1955 by the President and Fellows of Harvard College. Copyright © renewed 1979, 1983 by the President and Fellows of Harvard College. Copyright © 1914, 1918, 1919, 1924, 1929, 1930, 1932, 1935, 1937, 1942, by Martha Dickinson Bianchi. Copyright © 1952, 1957, 1958, 1963, 1965, by Mary L. Hampson. Used by permission. All rights reserved.

Chapter 11

1. "Gift of Finest Wheat." Text by Omer Westendorf, Music by Robert Kreutz. Text and music © 1977, Archdiocese of Philadelphia. Published exclusively by International Liturgy Publications. Used with permission.

Chapter 12

1. This information is sourced from Scott Neuman, "Fewer Than Half of U.S. Adults Belong to a Religious Congregation, New Poll Shows," *MPR News*, March 30, 2021, accessed July 2, 2022, https://www.npr.org/2021/03/30/982671783 /fewer-than-half-of-u-s-adults-belong-to-a-religious-congregation-new-poll -shows.

2. This information is sourced from Courtney Mares, "Why Do Some Young People Leave the Church? A New Study Investigates," *Catholic News Agency*, January 17, 2018, accessed July 2, 2022, https://www.catholicnewsagency .com/news/37533/why-do-some-young-people-leave-the-church-a-new-study -investigates.

3. This information is sourced from "Preaching Must Awaken Souls, Not Put Them to Sleep, Pope Says," *Catholic News Service*, January 27, 2022, accessed July 2, 2022, https://www.archstl.org/preaching-must-awaken-souls-not-put -them-to-sleep-pope-says-7261.

Epilogue

1. "When in Our Music God Is Glorified." Words: Fred Pratt Green. © 1972 Hope Publishing Company, www.hopepublishing.com. All rights reserved. Used by permission.